Collins

YOUR Life

CO-ORDINATOR'S FILE

KS3

WITH CD-ROM

JOHN FOSTER

William Collins' dream of knowledge for all began with the publication of his first book in 1819. A self-educated mill worker, he not only enriched millions of lives, but also founded a flourishing publishing house. Today, staying true to this spirit, Collins books are packed with inspiration, innovation and a practical expertise. They place you at the centre of a world of possibility and give you exactly what you need to explore it.

Collins. Do more.

Published by Collins
An imprint of HarperCollins*Publishers*
77–85 Fulham Palace Road
Hammersmith
London
W6 8JB

Browse the complete Collins catalogue at
www.collinseducation.com

10 9 8 7 6 5 4 3 2

ISBN-13 978-0-00-719847-4
ISBN-10 0-00-719847-7

John Foster asserts his moral right to be identified as the author of this work

British Library Cataloguing in Publication Data. A Catalogue record for this publication is available from the British Library

Commissioned by Thomas Allain-Chapman
Managed by Abigail Woodman
Project managed by Nancy Candlin
Edited by Liz Miles
Design and layout by Ken Vail Graphic Design, Cambridge
Cover design by bluepig
Cover photograph: Pixland/Bruno Coste
Production by Katie Butler
Printed and bound by Martins the Printers Ltd, Berwick upon Tweed

Acknowledgements:
Many thanks to all those teachers who responded to our call for feedback on what would give them greater freedom to teach in Citizenship and PSHE at Key Stage 3. And a special thank you to Gloria Nimenko, and Kim Briggs and her team at Norton Kanes High School, Cannock, who have read and commented on this Co-ordinator's File.

Adobe and Acrobat are trademarks of Adobe Systems Incorporated.

Contents

Preface

Your Life was among the first resources to be published to support the new Citizenship Programme of Study and the National Framework for PSHE published as part of the National Curriculum revisions in 2000. It has also been one of the most widely used, with over 1000 schools adopting the course.

In 2003, HarperCollins, the publishers, decided to find out what else those who had been using the course – as well as those who had not – needed to resource Citizenship and PSHE now that they had some experience of the new curriculum. They asked over 500 teachers and co-ordinators to explain what they felt were the key strengths of the course. Here are a few of the overwhelmingly positive responses received:

> *"Well planned, clearly written with useful suggestions for follow-up work and developmental work. User-friendly for pupils and teachers."*

> *"Relevant topics. Not patronising. Variety of approaches. Good design and layout. Age-appropriate activities and discussion points."*

> *"Well-presented, accessible materials which we can dip into to support our teaching. They are also invaluable when having to set cover work."*

> *"Carefully structured for non-specialist to use. User-friendly for pupils. Up-to-date info and lots of activities in each section. Teacher's guide – good supplement."*

HarperCollins also asked teachers currently using a variety of resources about what developments or supplements they would like to see in future, and this Co-ordinator's File is part of a range of revised and new components designed to respond to many of the requirements identified.

The most significant needs were for:

- **suggested lesson plans:** With the requirements of non-specialist and cover staff in mind, this File contains adaptable lesson plans for every spread in the *Your Life* student's books, complete with explicit curriculum links and learning objectives.

- **starter activities:** Suggestions for lesson/topic starters are included in the lesson plans, and are also a key component of the interactive CD-ROMs (see below).

- **more help with differentiation:** This File contains guidance on adapting the resources for SEN pupils, and the lesson plans have been constructed with the requirements of mixed ability and lower ability groups in mind. Further resources to support this work are also under consideration.

- **assessment and recording guidance and materials:** As well as assessment copymasters for all Citizenship units, the lesson plans in this File also identify key opportunities for assessment in PSHE. In addition, there are templates to support self-assessment and recording in PSHE and Citizenship in line with Ofsted requirements.

- **ICT resources:** This File contains guidance on integrating ICT into Citizenship and PSHE, in particular using the range of *Interactive Starters CD-ROMs* developed in conjunction with this publication.

- ***Your Life* for Years 10 and 11 (14–16):** Many teachers felt that a year-by-year course would be equally useful at Key Stage 4. More details of the extended *Your Life* course can be found on the inside front cover.

Whether you have been using *Your Life* since the outset or you are looking at it for the first time, I hope that you find this resource – and the revised and extended *Your Life* range – a practical and positive tool in developing and improving the quality of teaching and learning in both Citizenship and PSHE.

John Foster

How to use this file

The Co-ordinator's File is designed to provide materials that the PSHCE Key Stage 3 co-ordinator and their Year 7, 8 and 9 team leaders can give to individual teachers to help them use the *Your Life* books to deliver effective personal, social and health education and citizenship lessons. The bulk of the file, therefore, consists of ideas for lesson plans – between two and four for each of the units in the course, depending on the length of the unit.

There is an introductory section, illustrating how the three *Your Life* books meet the requirements of the Key Stage 3 National Curriculum Programme of Study for Citizenship and the Key Stage 3 National Framework for PSHE, and explaining how the lesson plans are structured to enable them to be adapted to fit a school's own timetable, depending upon how PSHCE is delivered within a particular school.

The Introduction also contains advice on how continuous assessment can be carried out and how students can reflect upon, record and evaluate what they have learned from each part of the course. Two other sections offer suggestions for helping students with special educational needs and on how ICT can be used as part of the *Your Life* course.

Each lesson plan is presented on a single sheet, so that it can be duplicated and given to individual members of the Year team. The lesson plans indicate clearly which part of either the Citizenship or PSHE framework guidelines are being covered and state the objective of the lesson. Each one begins with a Starter and contains suggestions for a range of activities and for a Plenary session. There are also suggestions for Extension activities, many of which involve the use of ICT.

Co-ordinators can use the lesson plans in two ways. Either they can be circulated at a planning meeting with the appropriate Year team members present and, after discussion, adapted to suit the needs of their particular classes or, alternatively, they can be distributed to individual teachers. In the latter case, the teacher is offered a quick and easy guide to planning their PSHCE lesson, albeit without the opportunity for joint planning.

The file also provides the co-ordinator with the means to ensure that there is assessment of the Citizenship strand of the course, by providing an Assessment copymaster for each of the Citizenship units of the course. Further opportunities for assessment, of both the Citizenship and PSHE strands of the course, are indicated in the lesson plans.

The 12 Recording and evaluation copymasters are designed to encourage the students to reflect on what they have learned at the end of each unit. They will prove most effective if used at the conclusion of each unit, rather than on a termly or half-termly basis.

The enclosed CD-ROM contains PDF files of all the lesson plans and copymasters, so you either print, photocopy or adapt them – whichever is easiest. In order to use these files you must have Adobe Acrobat Reader installed. Put the CD-ROM into your CD-ROM drive and, if you are using a PC, double-click on the CD-ROM drive icon inside My Computer. Or, if you are using a MAC, double-click on the CD-ROM icon on your desktop. Then double-click on the file you want to use.

How the *Your Life* course meets the requirements of the KS3 National Curriculum Programme of Study for Citizenship

The National Curriculum Programme of study for Citizenship at Key Stage 3 requires that knowledge and understanding about becoming informed citizens are acquired and applied when developing skills of enquiry and communication, and through participation and responsible action. The particular units of *Your Life 1–3* that meet the specific requirements of each Programme of Study are detailed below:

Knowledge and understanding about becoming informed citizens

1a	the legal and human rights and responsibilities underpinning society, basic aspects of the criminal justice system, and how both relate to young people		
	Your Life 1	Unit 5	You and your values – right and wrong
		Unit 8	You and the law – children's rights
		Unit 13	You and the community – being a good neighbour
		Unit 16	You as a citizen – Britain's government
	Your Life 2	Unit 8	You and the law – the police
	Your Life 3	Unit 5	You and your values – human rights issues
		Unit 8	You and the law – crimes and punishments
1b	the diversity of national, regional, religious and ethnic identities in the United Kingdom and the need for mutual respect and understanding		
	Your Life 1	Unit 3	You and your responsibilities – beliefs, customs and festivals
		Unit 5	You and your values – right and wrong
	Your Life 2	Unit 3	You and your responsibilities – other cultures and lifestyles
	Your Life 3	Unit 2	You and your responsibilities – racism, prejudice and discrimination
1c	central and local government, the public services they offer and how they are financed, and the opportunities to contribute		
	Your Life 1	Unit 16	You as a citizen – Britain's government
	Your Life 3	Unit 13	You and the community – local government and local organisations
1d	the key characteristics of parliamentary and other forms of government		
	Your Life 1	Unit 16	You as a citizen – Britain's government
	Your Life 3	Unit 14	You and your opinions – which political party do you support?
1e	the electoral system and the importance of voting		
	Your Life 1	Unit 16	You as a citizen – Britain's government
	Your Life 3	Unit 14	You and your opinions – which political party do you support?

1f	the work of community-based, national and international voluntary groups		
	Your Life 1	Unit 17	You and the community – taking action: raising money for a charity
	Your Life 2	Unit 17	You and the community – taking action on the local environment
	Your Life 3	Unit 5	You and your values – human rights issues
		Unit 17	You and the community – pressure groups and campaigning

1g	the importance of resolving conflict fairly		
	Your Life 3	Unit 16	You as a citizen of the world

1h	the significance of the media in society		
	Your Life 1	Unit 10	You and the media – the power of television
	Your Life 2	Unit 3	You and your responsibilities – other cultures and lifestyles
		Unit 10	You and the media – the power of advertising
	Your Life 3	Unit 10	You and the media – the power of the press
		Unit 17	You and the community – pressure groups and campaigning

1i	the world as a global community, and the political, economic, environmental and social implications of this, and the role of the European Union, the Commonwealth and the United Nations		
	Your Life 1	Unit 19	You and global issues – resources, waste and recycling
	Your Life 2	Unit 16	You as a citizen – of the European Union
		Unit 19	You and global issues – food and water
	Your Life 3	Unit 5	You and your values – human rights issues
		Unit 16	You as a citizen – of the world
		Unit 19	You and global issues – poverty

Developing skills of enquiry and communication

2a	to think about topical political, spiritual, moral, social and cultural issues, problems and events by analysing information and its sources, including ICT-based sources		
	Your Life 1	Unit 14	You and your opinions – how to express your ideas
	Your Life 2	Unit 5	You and your values – where do you stand?
		Unit 14	You and your opinions – speaking your mind

2b	to justify orally and in writing a personal opinion about such issues, problems or events		
	Your Life 1	Unit 14	You and your opinions – how to express your ideas
	Your Life 2	Unit 5	You and your values – where do you stand?
		Unit 14	You and your opinions – speaking your mind

2c	to contribute to group and exploratory class discussions and take part in debates		
	Your Life 1	Unit 14	You and your opinions – how to express your ideas
	Your Life 2	Unit 14	You and your opinions – speaking your mind

Note: In addition, all the other Citizenship units in *Your Life 1– 3* involve activities that will assist in the development of the students' skills of enquiry and communication.

Developing skills of participation and responsible action

3a	to use their imagination to consider other people's experiences and be able to think about, express and explain views that are not their own		
	Your Life 1	Unit 18	You and other people – people with disabilities
	Your Life 2	Unit 18	You and other people – older people
	Your Life 3	Unit 2	You and your responsibilities – racism, prejudice and discrimination
		Unit 5	You and your values – human rights issues
		Unit 19	You and global issues – poverty
3b	to negotiate, decide and take part responsibly in both school and community-based activities		
	Your Life 1	Unit 13	You and the community – being a good neighbour
		Unit 17	You and the community – taking action: raising money for a charity
		Unit 19	You and global issues – resources, waste and recycling
	Your Life 2	Unit 13	You and the community – the school as a community
		Unit 17	You and the community – taking action on the local environment
	Your Life 3	Unit 17	You and the community – pressure groups and campaigning
3c	to reflect on the process of participating		
	Your Life 1	Unit 17	You and the community – taking action: raising money for a charity
	Your Life 2	Unit 13	You and the community – the school as a community
		Unit 17	You and the community – taking action on the local environment
	Your Life 3	Unit 17	You and the community – pressure groups and campaigning

How the *Your Life* course meets the requirements of the KS3 National Framework for PSHE

The National Framework for PSHE details the knowledge, skills and understanding that students should develop at Key Stage 3. The particular units of *Your Life 1–3*, which help students to develop their self-knowledge, a healthy lifestyle and good relationships, are detailed below.

Developing confidence and responsibility and making the most of their abilities

1a	to reflect on and assess their strengths in relation to personality, work and leisure		
	Your Life 1	Unit 4	You and your time – managing your time
		Unit 20	You and your achievements – reviewing your progress
	Your Life 2	Unit 1	You and your feelings – self-esteem
		Unit 11	You and your time – making the most of your leisure
		Unit 20	You and your achievements – reviewing your progress
	Your Life 3	Unit 1	You and your body – adolescence
		Unit 3	You and your decisions – how to make decisions
		Unit 20	You and your achievements – reviewing your progress
1b	to respect the differences between people as they develop their own sense of identity		
	Your Life 1	Unit 9	You and other people – bullying
	Your Life 3	Unit 9	You and other people – being assertive
1c	to recognise how others see them, and be able to give and receive constructive feedback and praise		
	Your Life 2	Unit 1	You and your feelings – self-esteem
	Your Life 3	Unit 1	You and your body – adolescence
		Unit 9	You and other people – being assertive
1d	to recognise the stages of emotions associated with loss and change caused by death, divorce, separation and new family members, and how to deal positively with the strength of their feelings in different situations		
	Your Life 1	Unit 1	You and your feelings – anxieties and worries
	Your Life 2	Unit 6	You and your family – divided families
	Your Life 3	Unit 1	You and your body – adolescence
		Unit 6	You and your feelings – dealing with loss
1e	to relate job opportunities to their personal qualifications and skills, and understand how the choices they will make at Key Stage 4 should be based not only on knowledge of their personal strengths and aptitudes, but also on the changing world of work		
1f	to plan realistic targets for Key Stage 4, seeking out information and asking for help with career plans		
	Your Life 3	Unit 20	You and your achievements – reviewing your progress

1g	what influences how we spend or save money and how to become competent at managing personal money		
	Your Life 1	Unit 11	You and your money – pocket money, budgeting and saving
	Your Life 2	Unit 4	You and your money – gambling
	Your Life 3	Unit 11	You and your money – banking and ways of saving

Developing a healthy, safer lifestyle

2a	to recognise the physical and emotional changes that take place at puberty and how to manage these changes in a positive way		
	Your Life 1	Unit 2	You and your body – growing and changing
	Your Life 2	Unit 1	You and your feelings – self-esteem
	Your Life 3	Unit 1	You and your body – adolescence
2b	how to keep healthy and what influences health, including the media		
	Your Life 1	Unit 7	You and your body – smoking
		Unit 15	You and your body – eating and exercise
	Your Life 3	Unit 12	You and your body – eating disorders
2c	that good relationships and an appropriate balance between work, leisure and exercise can promote physical and mental health		
	Your Life 2	Unit 11	You and your time – making the most of your leisure
	Your Life 3	Unit 1	You and your body – adolescence
		Unit 18	You and other people – people with mental illnesses
2d	basic facts and laws, including school rules, about alcohol and tobacco, illegal substances and the risks of misusing prescribed drugs		
	Your Life 1	Unit 7	You and your body – smoking
		Unit 12	You and your body – drugs and drugtaking
	Your Life 2	Unit 2	You and your body – drugs and drugtaking
		Unit 12	You and your body – drinking and alcohol
	Your Life 3	Unit 7	You and your body – drugs and drugtaking
2e	in a context of the importance of relationships, about human reproduction, contraception, sexually transmitted infections, HIV and high-risk behaviours including early sexual activity		
	Your Life 2	Unit 15	You and your body – contraception and safer sex
	Your Life 3	Unit 15	You and your body – safer sex, STIs and AIDS

2f	to recognise and manage risk and make safer choices about healthy lifestyles, different environments and travel		
	Your Life 2	Unit 7	You and your safety – at home and in the street
		Unit 12	You and your body – drinking and alcohol
		Unit 14	You and your opinions – speaking your mind
	Your Life 3 Unit 12		You and your body – eating disorders

2g	to recognise when pressure from others threatens their personal safety and well-being, and to develop effective ways of resisting pressures, including knowing when and where to get help		
	Your Life 1	Unit 7	You and your body – smoking
	Your Life 2	Unit 2	You and your body – drugs and drugtaking
		Unit 7	You and your safety – at home and in the street

2h	basic emergency aid procedures and where to get help and support		
	Your Life 2	Unit 7	You and your safety – at home and in the street
	Your Life 3	Unit 7	You and your body – drugs and drugtaking

Developing good relationships and respecting the differences between people

3a	about the effects of all types of stereotyping, prejudice, bullying, racism and discrimination and how to challenge them assertively		
	Your Life 1	Unit 9	You and other people – bullying
		Unit 18	You and other people – people with disabilities
	Your Life 2	Unit 3	You and your responsibilities – other cultures and lifestyles
		Unit 18	You and other people – older people
	Your Life 3	Unit 2	You and your responsibilities – racism, prejudice and discrimination
		Unit 9	You and other people – being assertive

3b	how to empathise with people different from themselves		
	Your Life 1	Unit 18	You and other people – people with disabilities
	Your Life 2	Unit 9	You and other people – friends and friendships
		Unit 18	You and other people – older people
	Your Life 3	Unit 2	You and your responsibilities – racism, prejudice and discrimination

3c	about the nature of friendship and how to make and keep friends		
	Your Life 2	Unit 1	You and your feelings – self-esteem
		Unit 9	You and other people – friends and friendships
	Your Life 3	Unit 6	You and your feelings – dealing with loss

3d	to recognise some of the cultural norms in society, including the range of lifestyles and relationships		
	Your Life 2	Unit 3	You and your responsibilities – other cultures and lifestyles

3e	the changing nature of, and pressure on, relationships with friends and family, and when and how to seek help		
	Your Life 1	Unit 6	You and your family – getting on with others
	Your Life 2	Unit 6	You and your family – divided families
	Your Life 3	Unit 1	You and your body – adolescence
		Unit 4	You and your family – becoming an adult
		Unit 6	You and your feelings – dealing with loss

3f	about the role and importance of marriage in family relationships		
	Your Life 2	Unit 6	You and your family – divided families

3g	about the role and feelings of parents and carers and the value of family life		
	Your Life 1	Unit 6	You and your family – getting on with others
	Your Life 2	Unit 6	You and your family – divided families
	Your Life 3	Unit 4	You and your family – becoming an adult

3h	to recognise that goodwill is essential to positive and constructive relationships		
	Your Life 1	Unit 6	You and your family – getting on with others
	Your Life 3	Unit 4	You and your family – becoming an adult

3i	to negotiate within relationships, recognising that actions have consequences, and when and how to make compromises		
	Your Life 1	Unit 6	You and your family – getting on with others
	Your Life 3	Unit 3	You and your decisions – how to make decisions
		Unit 4	You and your family – becoming an adult
		Unit 9	You and other people – being assertive

3j	to resist pressure to do wrong, to recognise when others need help and how to support them		
	Your Life 1	Unit 9	You and other people – bullying
	Your Life 2	Unit 9	You and other people – friends and friendships
	Your Life 3	Unit 2	You and your responsibilities – racism, prejudice and discrimination
		Unit 3	You and your decisions – how to make decisions

3k	to communicate confidently with their peers and adults		
	Your Life 2	Unit 9	You and other people – friends and friendships
	Your Life 3	Unit 2	You and your responsibilities – racism, prejudice and discrimination
		Unit 4	You and your family – becoming an adult
		Unit 9	You and other people – being assertive

Planning and delivering PSHE and Citizenship lessons

Planning the course

The *Your Life* books together meet the requirements for PSHE and Citizenship at Key Stage 3 (see pages 7–13). Using the *Your Life* books as the core of a course, therefore, ensures that a school is not only covering the statutory requirement for Citizenship, but also the framework guidelines for PSHE. Specific units included in the 'Keeping healthy' strand of the course also provide appropriate sex and relationships education that can be incorporated into a school's own sex education policy. Similarly, there are units in the 'Understanding yourself' strand designed to develop students' awareness of themselves and their aptitudes as part of the school's careers and guidance programme.

As the units in each of the books are divided into four strands ('Understanding yourself', 'Keeping healthy', 'Developing relationships' and 'Developing as a citizen), it is possible to plan to deliver the course strand by strand. This arrangement may suit schools in which the PSHCE course is being delivered by a team of teachers with expertise in different areas. However, the units within each strand are freestanding and can, therefore, be delivered in any order. Schools can either plan to use the units in whatever sequence they choose or, alternatively, use them in the order in which they appear in the books. Whatever the school may decide, there is sufficient material in each book to provide the basis for a full year's course.

Planning a unit

Each of the units in *Your Life 1, 2* and *3* covers a specific area of either the PSHE or Citizenship curriculum in two to four lessons. The lessons within a unit are planned so that there is a clear progression in the building of the student's knowledge and understanding of the topic. Thus in Unit 9 of *Your Life 1*, the first lesson explores what bullying is and who gets bullied, the second lesson explains why people bully and what it feels like to be bullied and the third lesson examines the different ways of reacting to bullying and discusses what to do if you are being bullied. Similarly, in Unit 12 of *Your Life 2*, the first lesson presents information on the effects of drinking alcohol, and on teenage drinking and the laws about alcohol, leading to an exploration in the second lesson of the problems that excessive drinking can cause.

It is important that the PSHCE co-ordinator draws the attention of the teachers in their team to these links between lessons at the start of a unit. It is, therefore, suggested that the lesson plans are distributed to teachers unit-by-unit rather than lesson-by-lesson.

Using the lesson plans

Each lesson plan is presented on a separate sheet, so that it can easily be duplicated and distributed to teachers. The lesson plans all have the same structure so that they are easy to follow:

- The learning **Objective** is stated, so that it can be made clear to the students. It can be written up on the board and explained at the beginning, and referred to during the lesson. If it is the second, third or fourth lesson of a unit, it can be explained how the learning objective links to and follows on from the previous lesson(s) and how it is related to any subsequent lesson(s).

- Details are given of any **Resources** that are required for the activities. These are mainly optional. Often, the only resource needed is one of the copymasters from the *Teacher's Resources*, and then only if the teacher decides to incorporate one of the suggested extension activities into the main lesson.

- A short **Starter** activity is suggested as a way in to the topic. These take a variety of forms. In many instances, the starter activity involves asking the students to do a brainstorm (e.g. to suggest the reasons why people gamble), with the teacher listing their ideas on the board. A detailed exploration of the question follows during the main part of the lesson. Another type of starter activity asks the students to draw on their own experiences. For example, in the lesson on safety in the home, students are asked to share their experiences of accidents in the home, explaining what caused them and whether anyone was on hand who was able to give first aid. Other starter activities involve the explanation of key terms, such as 'stereotyping' and 'discrimination', and writing definitions of them on the board. Often, it is possible to incorporate the explanation of the learning objective as part of the starter activity. The length of time allocated to the starter activity will obviously vary, depending on the activity, but typically it is expected to last about five minutes.

- There are **Suggested activities** for the main part of the lesson. Many of the activities involve the students studying an article prior to discussing it in pairs or groups, then sharing their ideas in a class discussion. Others present the students with test-yourself quizzes, e.g. about their homework habits, or ask them to consider different ways of behaving in a particular situation by performing role plays. There are also suggestions for writing activities, ranging from making lists and writing letters to designing leaflets and producing a Year 8 newsletter.

  There are sufficient suggestions to fill an hour's lesson. However, the length of the PSHCE lesson varies from school to school, and in many cases may be less than an hour. Therefore, when planning the lesson, teachers may have to select which of the suggested activities to include. Obviously, the more activities that are completed, the more comprehensively a topic will be covered. But in the majority of the lessons it is not essential for all the activities to be done in order for the learning objective to be achieved.

- There is a **Plenary** activity designed to round off the lesson by drawing attention to what has been learned. This is usually an oral activity, during which the teacher may summarise the main points of the lesson in some way, e.g. by asking the class to say what key messages they would try to put across as part of a campaign to warn about the risks of drugtaking, and writing their suggestions on the board. The aim of the plenary activity is to review and reinforce the learning that has taken place in the main body of the lesson.

- For each lesson, there are a number of **Extension activities**. These provide activities that can be done either within the main lesson as additional activities or set as follow-up work. This section includes the activities that can be developed using the copymasters provided in the *Teacher's Resources*. It also contains suggestions for activities that require more time than a single lesson to complete, e.g. for the extended writing of a magazine article and the holding of a mock election. There are also research activities with details of websites that the students can visit in order to find more information on the topic.

- In one of the lesson plans for each of the Citizenship units of the course, there is an **Assessment** section referring to the Assessment copymaster (e.g. 7A) that can be used as part of the lesson to assess the students' knowledge and understanding and/or skills.

- At the end of the final lesson of each unit, there is a **Recording and evaluating (R/E)** section, referring to the Reviewing and recording copymasters (e.g. R5) that can be given to students so that they can reflect on and record what they have learned.

Developing group discussions

Many of the activities in the *Your Life* course involve groups in discussing issues and sharing opinions, thus providing individuals with an opportunity to consider various viewpoints and develop their own ideas. It is important, therefore, not only to set out ground rules for discussion in order to ensure that students respect each other's feelings and views, but also to ensure that the discussion remains focused and is conducted in an orderly way.

A useful way of setting up the ground rules is to involve the students themselves in doing so as part of an introductory lesson at the beginning of the course, in which the teacher explains the aims and purpose of the course and the type of work they will be doing. The class can be split into groups and each group given a large sheet of paper. They can then be invited to suggest the kind of rules that are needed in order to make sure that a discussion in class is successful, so that everyone can say what they think without fear of being ridiculed or feeling embarrassed, so that people can listen to other people's points of view, and so that everyone can participate in the discussion. The groups can then be asked to report their suggestions to the rest of the class and the class can work together to agree a list of ground rules, which the teacher can write on the board. A member of the class can then type the ground rules on a word processor and print them out, so that each person has a copy of them in their PSHCE file. An enlarged copy can be printed out and put on display in the classroom.

If groups are to conduct their discussions in an orderly fashion, someone must ensure that the ground rules are adhered to. One of the keys to successful group discussions is to make the class aware of the importance of appointing someone to chair the discussion, and of the key role of the chairperson. Explain that it is the responsibility of the chairperson to organise and control the discussion. The characteristics of a good chairperson are explained on page 64 of *Your Life 1* and it is suggested that the lesson on group discussions on pages 64–65 is included early in the course. The lesson also includes guidelines for individuals on how to participate in group discussions and the points made in these guidelines can be compared to those in the class's ground rules.

One of the problems of group discussions is keeping the groups focused on the task. One way of doing this is to ask each group to appoint a secretary. The role of the secretary is to keep track of any decisions made by the group or of the main opinions expressed in the group. Many students will find this a difficult role to fill, as it requires the person not only to listen carefully to what is said and to pick out and summarise the main points, but also to write them down. However, requiring someone in the group to write something down, albeit in note form, is often an effective way of ensuring that the group remains on-task.

Alternatively, the group can appoint a reporter, whose role is to report the group's ideas at the start of a follow-up class discussion. While this requires the same listening and summarising skills as the secretary's role, it avoids the need for any writing. Formalising how a group report their ideas to the rest of the class by encouraging them to appoint a reporter is another way of helping to keep them on task.

Keeping a PSHCE file

It is recommended that the students are given a file at the beginning of the first year of the course and that they build up the file over the three years. The file could include:

- a copy of the course programme – this might be a copy of the *Your Life 1–3* grid, showing the four different strands of the course, and/or copies of the National Curriculum Programme of Study for Citizenship and the National Framework for PSHE for Key Stage 3, or a copy of the school's own course programme. Having a copy of the course in their file means that students can understand how the lessons meet the requirements of the curriculum;

- reference sheets, such as the ground rules for group discussions (see above);

- written work completed during the course, including assessments (see page 17);

- information and advice leaflets, e.g. on drugs, first aid;

- recording and evaluation sheets (see page 17).

The file can thus provide a record of what has been covered and learned during the PSHCE course for teachers, students and their parents.

Assessment, recording and evaluation

Assessment

Continuous assessment forms an important and integral part of the *Your Life* course. To facilitate the assessment of the Citizenship strand, which is a required part of the curriculum, the file contains 24 Assessment copymasters – one for each of the Citizenship units in the course. These take a variety of forms, ranging from multiple-choice tests and true/false quizzes to crosswords and word puzzles, the writing of checklists and producing flowcharts or step-by-step guidelines.

The copymasters are designed to assess students' knowledge and understanding, and/or their skills, rather than their attitudes and values. While it is feasible to test the students' skills at expressing their views, a PSHCE course can only have objectives to equip students with the information on which to base their opinions and to develop their skills of decision-making, rather than to make up their minds for them and to tell them what to think.

While assessment of PSHE is not mandatory, many of the activities, which are included in the PSHE strands of the course, provide opportunities for assessment. These are indicated, wherever they occur, within the lesson plans with the symbol **AO** and there is at least one assessment opportunity per unit. The Citizenship units also contain a number of other opportunities for assessment, in addition to the assessment activities contained on the copymasters, and these too are noted in the lesson plans.

Often it is a writing activity, following the reading of an article and/or a group or class discussion of an issue, which provides the opportunity for assessment. This may be a straightforward test of knowledge, e.g. in Unit 7 of *Your Life 1* students are asked to design a leaflet on 'Ten Things You Should Know About Smoking' and in Unit 15 of *Your Life 3* they have to design an internet web page giving key information about HIV and AIDS. Alternatively, the writing activity may involve demonstrating understanding, e.g. of how to cope with difficult feelings by writing a letter to someone who is upset at having to go and live in a stepfamily (Unit 6 of *Your Life 2*) or of the causes of arguments between brothers and sisters and how to help family members get on better (Unit 4 of *Your Life 3*).

However, it is important that there should be oral assessments as well as written assessments, so that all students can be assessed whatever their literacy skills. Many of the writing activities could be adapted and done orally. For example, where students are asked to write a letter, they could give a verbal explanation of what the letter would contain.

Throughout the course, there are many suggestions for students to share what they have learned in class discussions. These, too, can be used for assessment. For example, in Unit 2 of *Your Life 3* there is the opportunity to assess their understanding of an article on racial discrimination during a class discussion.

Role plays also offer the chance to assess students' understanding and skills, e.g. the role play at handling peer pressure to join in and do something they do not want to do in Unit 2 in *Your Life 2* can be used to assess their understanding of strategies for saying 'No'. Similarly, the role play in Unit 9 of *Your Life 3* can be used to assess their understanding of the difference between assertive, aggressive and passive behaviour.

Whenever an assessment is being made, it is suggested that the students are informed. The more a school shows that it values what students are learning in PSHCE lessons by making students aware that their learning is being assessed, the more highly the students are likely to value the course.

Reviewing and recording students' learning

An important component of the PSHE/Citizenship course is that students should reflect on what they have learned during the course. To facilitate this reflection, there are four 'Reviewing and recording your learning' copymasters for each year of the course. Each of the copymasters focuses on reviewing and recording the learning outcomes that have resulted from the study of the units in one particular strand, e.g. 'Developing as a citizen'.

The copymasters can be put in the student's file at the beginning of the year and a comment written in the appropriate space following the completion of a unit. Alternatively, they can be distributed and completed as part of the end-of-year assessment and recording process. The advantages of having them completed at the end of each unit is that the learning outcomes are fresh in the student's mind at that point and thus they will find it easier to reflect on their learning. Another advantage of making the process of reflection on-going is that there will always be an up-to-date record in the student's file, which can be made available to parents at parent's consultations.

Supporting students with special educational needs

Teaching methods and learning styles

Using varied teaching methods and learning styles helps to provide teachers with opportunities to address students' individual needs in the classroom and to support students with special educational needs more effectively. This file suggests a variety of teaching methods and learning styles, and these methods, coupled with good SEN practice in the classroom, can provide effective support to include students of all abilities in PSHCE lessons.

Other strategies to support needs

Differentiating resources

Some of the suggested writing activities in this file may need to be differentiated in order to cater for the different levels of need in the classroom. This can be done in a variety of ways by:

- breaking down writing tasks into more manageable chunks, allowing students to deal with writing tasks more easily, e.g. writing frames can be used to give structure to some of the tasks suggested, such as writing a story, letter, article, diary, making notes, fact sheet, articles and replies;
- presenting complementary, adapted resources that cater for the different ability levels in the group;
- pitching group activities at different levels to cater for the varying ability levels in the group;
- providing more complex activities to stretch the more able students – there are a variety of extension activities that would provide appropriate work for some of the more able learners.

Using peer support

In the activities where pupils are required to read information individually prior to discussion, teachers can make use of peer support, e.g. a teacher can pair a good reader with a weaker reader. Using peer support in this way can also be extended to group work, with the teacher structuring the groups so that there is at least one good reader in each group. Group-reading activities require careful structuring to make sure that all students with lower reading ages do not go into one group.

Supporting pupils with specific learning difficulties

There are a variety of ways of achieving this, depending on each student's special educational needs, by:

- introducing new words explicitly, e.g. the starter activities often suggest writing key terms and definitions on the board;
- letting students present their work in a different way, thus making allowances for their special needs, e.g. completing a mind-map instead of writing a fact sheet, recording pair or group discussions instead of making notes on points discussed;
- encouraging students to use visual representations to make useful points (there are plenty of activities that provide opportunities for this, e.g. designing a poster, making a leaflet, watching a video);

- allowing students to present their ideas orally where possible, e.g. through spoken quizzes so that the students do not have to read the questions and during which pupils can also answer questions orally instead of writing their answers down;

- not presenting large amounts of text to students who have low reading ages (too much text will easily lead to frustration and boredom and will lower their self esteem);

- encouraging students to word process their work so that they can check grammar and spelling easily, as well as improving presentation (improving presentation can help to boost students' confidence and self esteem);

- using the *Your Life* multi-sensory interactive CD-ROMs at the beginning of lessons (these are visually interesting and interactive, and therefore provide multi-sensory experiences which are powerful learning aids for students with special educational needs);

- choosing appropriate activities from the file that suit the needs of the class and pupils with special educational needs;

- liaising with the SENCO to acquire information on pupils' reading ages in your groups, plus any additional information on pupils with special educational needs;

- reviewing the needs of the students with special education needs regularly to ensure their needs are being met in the PSHCE lessons.

Integrating learning support

Teacher assistants in the classroom provide a vital way of supporting and integrating students with special educational needs, e.g. by helping to clarify instructions; motivating and encouraging students in group work activities; assisting in weak areas such as language, behaviour, reading, spelling, planning and drafting writing activities; and by helping students to concentrate and complete tasks. In addition to this, they can help by establishing a supportive relationship with the students and in encouraging the acceptance and integration of students with special educational needs.

Good liaison between PSHCE staff and teaching assistants prior to lessons will enable pupils' needs are determined, as well as any resource implications such as devising complementary learning activities. Involving teacher assistants fully in the aims, content and strategies and outcomes will prove extremely effective in helping pupils with special educational needs to participate fully in the PSHCE lessons.

Using ICT in the *Your Life* course

Computers are a powerful learning tool in PSHCE lessons, as they are in many other areas of the curriculum.

ICT can be used in the *Your Life* course in a variety of ways.

Interactive Starters CD-ROMs

There is an Interactive Starters CD-ROM for Year 7, Year 8 and Year 9. Each CD-ROM contains an Interactive Starter for every unit in the corresponding student's book. In addition to this, there is a follow-up activity in the form of a PDF file for every unit and a booklet showing how the material can be used. The CD-ROMs are powerful learning aids in the PSHCE lessons, offering visually interesting and interactive activities, with multi-sensory experiences.

The CD-ROMs contain a variety of different activities to stimulate students' interest at the start of a PSHCE lesson:

Introductory presentations

- These present the students with key concepts, facts or viewpoints to lead into an interactive task. For example, facts about smoking are presented in a video clip to introduce Unit 7 of *Your Life 1*. This is followed by an interactive task consisting of multiple-choice questions. In Unit 9 of *Your Life 1* bullying issues are raised by presenting a series of situations for the students to discuss and to decide how they should react in each situation.

- **Voting activities:** A number of the interactive tasks involve the students in voting activities. For example, information about different charities is presented (Unit 17, *Your Life 1*) and students have to vote on which one to support. Other voting activities involve ranking exercises. For example, in Unit 5 of *Your Life 1* the class is presented with visual examples of antisocial behaviours and have to decide which is the most serious. They are then presented with a summary of their results.

- **Quizzes:** These provide an effective and enjoyable way for the class to investigate an issue. Animation and sound effects are used. All questions are multiple-choice based, with feedback for students on their performance in graphical and/or textual form. For example, in Unit 7 of *Your Life 2* there is a quiz about safety in the home.

- **Presentations:** Another type of activity involves the students in producing a report or presentation based on information they are given. For example, in Unit 2 of *Your Life 2* they are provided with information on ecstasy to enable them produce a report consisting not only of their textual input, but also of images and audio comments. Students are also able to interact with simulated situations to encourage them to explore the consequences of decisions.

The follow-up activities can also be copied and used as worksheets.

Using the Interactive Starters CD-ROMs

Ideally, use a suite of computers, allowing for whole-class interactive teaching. This will hold the class together and maximise participation. The teacher initially presents the activity, e.g. on an interactive whiteboard. The students can then work independently on the starter activity, with the teacher working with the class or individuals.

If there is a single or only a few computers in the classroom, the teacher can present the interactive CD-ROM to the whole class, while some students work in pairs or groups and take turns to use the CD-ROM(s).

Other ways of using ICT in the *Your Life* course

- Some activities suggested in this file require students to search for information on suggested websites related to the particular unit. This is a valuable way of helping to develop students' search skills. The students can store the website addresses and any useful images and information.

- Students can desk-top publish posters or leaflets that they have designed in the lessons, as well as any mind-maps that provide useful summaries for their PSHCE files.

- ICT can be used to finish activities outside of class time. This means that students can work at their own pace and when it suits them.

- Teachers or students can record role-play activities using a digital camera. These images can be stored and edited on a PC hard drive and can also be displayed on classroom or corridor notice boards.

- Word-processing makes writing tasks easier by highlighting spelling mistakes, which can be amended, and by alleviating any handwriting problems.

Developing effective links with the ICT department and finding other ways to use ICT in the lessons will help enhance the students' learning.

UNIT 1 You and your feelings – anxieties and worries

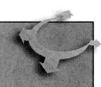

Your Life 1/Year 7

Lesson 1 *Your Life 1*, pages 6–7
National Framework for PSHE coverage 1d

Objective: To understand feelings of anxiety about school and to explore ways of dealing with such feelings.

Resources

Copies of the plan of the school and of the school rules

Copies of Copymaster 1 'Feeling stressed and unhappy' (*Your Life 1 Copymasters,* page 13)

Starter

Introduce the topic by asking the students to think about the things that have made them anxious during their first days at secondary school. Then read the advice on 'Settling in' (page 6). Which piece of advice do they think is the most useful?

Suggested activities

● Ask the students, in pairs, to familiarise themselves with: the school layout by studying the school plans; their timetables by discussing what they need to bring to school on particular days; and the school rules by discussing what particular rules there are, e.g. on school uniform. Conclude the activity with a class discussion about rules, why schools have them, and how rules make it possible for the school to operate as a community.

● Ask groups to decide who is the best person to help them in a crisis (see 'Students with problems', page 6), then share their views in a class discussion.

● Read 'Manjit's story' on page 7. Discuss how she overcame her anxiety. Then invite pairs to discuss the advice they would give to students with other anxieties, before acting out the role play.

Plenary

Discuss what the students have learned about feeling anxious and worried at school, and about particular problems and how to deal with them.

Extension activities

Ask students to write about their feelings about starting secondary school, describing their anxieties and worries, any problems they have faced and how they have dealt with them.

Hand out copies of Copymaster 1. By discussing the letters and advice and preparing their replies to Estelle's letter, the students can demonstrate their understanding of how to cope with anxieties and worries. They can then look for examples of similar letters in magazines and discuss the advice that is given.

Your Life 1/Year 7

UNIT 1 You and your feelings – anxieties and worries

Your Life 1/Year 7

Lesson 2 *Your Life 1*, pages 8–9
National Framework for PSHE coverage 1d

Objective: To understand how to deal with anxiety, in particular anxiety caused by feelings of rejection, shyness and grief.

Resources

Copies of Copymaster R1 'Understanding yourself' (page 181)

Starter

Discuss what it means to feel rejected, to feel a lack of confidence because of shyness and to feel grief. Talk about how each of these feelings can cause anxiety and how it is important to learn how to deal with them.

Suggested activities

- Read the three letters and the advice given in the article from *Shout* on page 8. Focus on each letter in turn. Encourage students who are willing to do so to share their own experiences of such feelings. Discuss how helpful they find the advice. What is the most useful piece of advice? What is the least useful? What other advice would they offer on how to deal with the anxieties caused by these feelings?

- Read the article 'Packing up your cares and woes' (page 9). Invite pairs and groups to discuss the questions about sharing their worries and to talk about whom they could share their worries with.

Plenary

Discuss what the class has learned about anxieties and how to deal with them in a class discussion. Emphasise the importance of sharing their worries if their anxiety is getting on top of them. Explain that if they do not feel they can talk to someone face to face, they can always telephone a helpline such as ChildLine (Freephone 0800 1111).

Extension activities

Ask the students to write a story about someone whose worries get on top of him or her. Explain that they could, if they wish, base it on their own experience of a time when they were anxious because of feelings of rejection, shyness or grief.

Explain what a counsellor does. If your school has a counsellor, ask them to talk to the students about their role. Suggest the students to use the internet to research counselling services that are available for young people.

Recording and evaluating

Ask the students to fill in the appropriate section of Copymaster R1, to record and evaluate what they learned from this unit.

UNIT 2 You and your body – growing and changing

Your Life 1/Year 7

Lesson 1 – *Your Life 1*, pages 10–11
National Framework for PSHE coverage 2a

Objective: To understand what puberty is, the physical changes that occur during puberty and what causes those changes.

Resources

Copies of Copymaster 2 'Periods' (*Your Life 1 Copymasters*, page 14)

Starter

Explain what puberty is and how the release of either female or male hormones causes a person's body to change during puberty. Ask the students how a girl's body changes and how a boy's body changes, and compile lists on the board.

Suggested activities

- Read the article 'Becoming a woman' (page 10). Ask groups to discuss the questions on the article and to compare the list the class made of how a girl's body changes with the list of changes described in the article.

- Invite individuals to prepare a reply to Christy's letter 'Am I normal?' (page 10), and then to use a computer to draft a reply.

- Read the article 'Becoming a man' (page 11). Ask groups to discuss the questions on the article and to compare their list of how a boy's body changes with the list of changes described in the article.

Plenary

Discuss how some people get embarrassed by the changes that happen to their bodies, and how others become worried because the changes occur later to their bodies than to the bodies of their friends. Emphasise that the changes are natural and nothing to get embarrassed about, that it is perfectly normal for the changes to happen to different people at different ages, and that it is hurtful to tease a person about the fact that their body has or has not changed. Finally, introduce the idea of the questions box ('Puberty problems', page 11) and explain how they can ask anonymously any question they would prefer not to ask publicly.

Extension activities

Discuss and answer the questions the students put into the box. Use any questions about periods as a way of introducing and discussing the information on Copymaster 2. Focus in particular on the advice that is given on how to cope with PMS and painful periods.

Students can find more information about what happens during puberty on the internet, e.g. at www.kidshealth.org/index.html, which includes an article entitled 'Everything you wanted to know about puberty – but felt weird asking'.

If your school has a nurse, ask him or her to talk to the students.

Your Life 1/Year 7

UNIT 2 You and your body – growing and changing

Your Life 1/Year 7

Lesson 2 *Your Life 1*, pages 12–13
National Framework for PSHE coverage 2a

Objective: To understand the emotional changes that take place at puberty and how to manage these changes in a positive way.

Resources

Copies of Copymaster R2 'Keeping healthy' (page 182)

Starter

Recap on what puberty is and explain that the increase in the levels of hormones causes changes in a person's feelings, as well as physical changes. Explain that someone can have positive feelings and negative feelings. Make lists on the board of positive and negative feelings and discuss how certain feelings, such as anger, can be positive or negative, depending on how they are dealt with. Explain to the class that the aim of this lesson is to help them to be able to recognise their feelings and to learn how to manage them.

Suggested activities

- Read the article 'Getting in touch with your feelings' (pages 12–13). Either ask the students to work in pairs, identifying what they consider to be the main points in the article, then discussing the points in groups or as a class; or work on the article with the whole class. The key things to focus on are the three basic rules stated in the middle section of the article (page 13).

- Ask groups to carry out the discussion activity on the four statements quoted on page 13, then to share their views in a class discussion. Focus in particular on the second statement, stressing the need to learn how to follow your feelings and to say "No" if you really don't want to join in and do something that everybody else wants you to do.

Plenary

Ask: "What have you learned about positive ways of dealing with your feelings, and negative ways of dealing with them?" Discuss how it is positive to be able to recognise the reasons for certain feelings, to let feelings out and to follow them when making decisions. Talk about how it is negative to wallow in feelings without exploring the reasons for them, to bottle up feelings, and to ignore them when taking action. Finally, remind the students of the types of feelings that are normal during puberty (see the end of the article on page 13) and how these are a normal part of growing up.

Extension activities

Challenge the students to do the role plays (see page 13) to demonstrate their skills at saying "No". Then hold a debriefing session to discuss how they felt when they said "No" and any difficulties they faced when doing so. Encourage them to discuss any strategies they may have used to help them to resist the pressure that the friend put on them.

Recording and evaluating

Ask students to fill in the appropriate section of Copymaster R2 to record and evaluate what they learned from this unit.

UNIT 3 You and your responsibilities – beliefs, customs and festivals

Your Life 1/Year 7

Lesson 1 *Your Life 1*, pages 14–15
National Curriculum Programme of Study for Citizenship coverage 1b; links with QCA exemplar unit 4

Objective: To understand that Britain is a diverse society, and that it is important to respect the wide variety of beliefs and customs which are part of life in Britain.

Starter

Read the introductory paragraph 'What do you believe?' (page 14). Discuss: "What influences your beliefs? Your family? Your neighbours? People who share your religion? Your school friends and school teachers? People who write the books you read? People you admire? Things you hear on television and the radio? Things you read in newspapers and magazines?"

Talk about the communities to which the students belong and how their views and beliefs are influenced by people in those communities and by the media.

Suggested activities

- Ask the students to study the list of statements under 'I believe' (page 14), to record their scores and to compare them in groups.

- Hold a class discussion and explain that people who belong to certain religions groups hold a number of the listed beliefs, e.g. many Muslims believe statements 2, 7, 8, 9 and 14. Many Jewish people believe statements 6 and 15. Many Jehovah's Witnesses believe statement 16. Conclude this discussion by stressing that in a diverse society people hold a wide range of different beliefs.

- Explain that dress customs may be based on beliefs. Read the story 'Rachel and Yasmeen' (page 15) and ask the students to discuss why Yasmeen is allowed to dress differently and why it is important that she should be allowed to do so.

Plenary

Write the words 'discrimination' and 'prejudice' on the board. Explain that prejudice means intolerance of, or dislike of, people who come from a particular race or who have particular beliefs. Explain that discrimination means the unfair treatment of a person or group of people based on prejudice.

Read 'Freedom from discrimination' (page 15). Discuss Mr Sagar's story and re-emphasise the importance of respecting different customs and beliefs.

Extension activity

Ask the students to write a paragraph to explain why it is important to respect other people's beliefs.

Your Life 1/Year 7

UNIT 3 You and your responsibilities – beliefs, customs and festivals

Your Life 1/Year 7

Lesson 2 *Your Life 1*, pages 16–17
National Curriculum Programme of Study for Citizenship coverage 1b; links with QCA exemplar unit 4

Objective: To understand how food customs can be based on religious beliefs and to research festivals based on religious beliefs.

Resources

Copies of Copymaster 3 'Obon' (*Your Life 1 Copymasters,* page 15)

Copies of Copymaster R3 'Developing relationships' (page 183)

Starter

Introduce the topic of food customs with a short discussion on vegetarianism. Encourage anyone in the class who is a vegetarian to explain why they are a vegetarian, if they wish to do so. Discuss how being a vegetarian and refusing to eat meat is often based on the belief that it is wrong for humans to eat animals.

Suggested activities

- In pairs, ask the students to read 'Jewish food laws' (page 16), then to perform the role play to show their understanding of how religious beliefs can determine what people eat.

- Read 'Salim comes to tea' (page 16) and ask groups to discuss the questions, then to report their views in a class discussion.

- Read the paragraph on 'Easter' (page 17) and either ask groups to draw up a calendar of Christian festivals or work together as a class to draw up the calendar. Be aware that students may find this difficult and will need to have many of the main days of the Christian calendar explained to them, e.g. Shrove Tuesday, Ash Wednesday, Palm Sunday, Good Friday, Easter, Whit Sunday.

Plenary

Recap what they have learned from the lesson about food customs based on religious beliefs. Read the paragraph on 'Janmashtami' (page 17) and set up the extension activity to research a religious festival.

Extension activities

Ask the students to work either individually or in pairs to research a religious festival, and to prepare a factsheet on it for a class 'A–Z of festivals'.

In groups, ask the class to study Copymaster 3, to discuss what they learn from it about Obon, and what message about people's religious beliefs is conveyed by Barrie Wade's poem. Then ask the students to share their views in a class discussion.

Recording and evaluating

Ask students to fill in the appropriate section of Copymaster R3 to record and evaluate what they have learned from this unit.

UNIT 4 You and your time – managing your time

Your Life 1/Year 7

Lesson 1 *Your Life 1*, pages 18–19
National Framework for PSHE coverage 1a

> **Objective:** To encourage students to assess their management of their time, and to help them to understand the importance of planning and organisation in their personal lives.

Resources

Copies of Copymaster 4 'How good are you at managing your time?' (*Your Life 1 Copymasters*, page 16)

Starter

Explain to students that the purpose of the lesson is to look at how they manage their time. Ask: "How well do you think you manage your time?" Ask them to give themselves a mark out of ten for their time-management and to explain the reasons why they gave themselves that mark.

Suggested activities

- Give out copies of the quiz and ask the students to complete the quiz on their own.

- In pairs, invite students to share what they have learned from the activity about how good they are at planning and organising their lives and making the best use of their time.

- Compare what the activity tells the class about their use of their time, with their own assessment of their use of time given in the Starter. Had they given themselves a true assessment? Do they need to alter the mark they gave themselves in the light of what the quiz has revealed?

- Together, study the list of 'Time-saving tips' (page 19), and then ask students to decide on up to three things each of them could do that would improve their management of time.

Plenary

Hold a class discussion, focusing on the time-saving tips. What other time-saving tips can they suggest? Which do they think are the most useful tips? List the tips on the board, then appoint someone to copy down the list and type it on computer for display on the classroom wall. You could print out copies for the students to put in their files, too.

Extension activity

Ask the students to write the letter to Darren, advising him on how to manage his time (see 'For your file' page 19), in order to demonstrate their understanding of how they can manage their time effectively.

Your Life 1/Year 7

UNIT 4 You and your time – managing your time

Your Life 1/Year 7

Lesson 2 *Your Life 1*, pages 20–21
National Framework for PSHE coverage 1a

> **Objective:** To explore homework habits and to discuss problems with homework and how best to handle them.

Resources

Copies of Copymaster R1 'Understanding yourself' (page 181)

Starter

Introduce the topic of homework by asking the class: "How good are you at getting your homework done?" Talk about problems with homework. Ask: "What is the main problem?" (Finding the time to do it? Forgetting what it is? Finding somewhere to do it? Not being able to do it? Getting interrupted all the time? Not being able to find the books/equipment needed? It taking so long that it can't be completed?) Make a list on the board of homework problems. Explain that the purpose of the lesson is to look at attitudes towards homework and how to deal with homework problems.

Suggested activities

- Read the views about homework of the four students (pages 20–21). You could invite four students to read aloud the statements of Salima, Tristan, Gary and Abby.

- Ask groups to discuss the follow-up questions on page 21 and to draw up a list of advice on how to cope with homework.

- Hold a class discussion in which the spokesperson from each group takes it in turn to report the group's ideas on how best to cope with homework.

- Ask pairs of students to study the list of homework problems (page 21) and to decide what advice they would give to each person. Encourage the students to share their ideas in a group or class discussion.

Plenary

As a class, make a list of 'Top Ten Tips on How to Handle Homework'. Either ask the class to copy out the list as you write it up on the board or ask someone to put the list on the computer, so that you can print copies for the students' files.

Extension activities

Invite the students to act out the role play (page 21) in which one of a group of friends refuses to give in to pressure to go out, and says that they have set aside the time to do their homework. Then hold a debriefing session to discuss how the person felt when saying "No" and what they can do in such situations to help them not give in to pressure.

A test-yourself quiz on homework habits can be found on pages 10–11 of *Studywise 1* (Collins Educational). You could make photocopies and students could use it to assess their homework habits.

Recording and evaluating

Ask students to fill in the appropriate section of Copymaster R1 to record and evaluate what they have learned from this unit.

UNIT 5 You and your values – right and wrong

Your Life 1/Year 7

Lesson 1 *Your Life 1*, pages 22–23
National Curriculum Programme of Study for Citizenship coverage 1a, 2a, 2b, 2c; links with QCA exemplar unit 3

Objective: To develop students' own sense of values and responsibility towards others by sharing their views on right and wrong behaviour and on the seriousness of various forms of antisocial behaviour.

Resources

Copies of Copymaster 5 'Which is most serious?' (*Your life 1 Copymasters,* page 17)

Copies of Copymaster 1A 'Understanding your values' (page 157)

Starter

Discuss how, as members of society, we all have responsibilities about how we behave, and how our behaviour depends on what we believe to be right and wrong. Talk about how members of religious communities have guidelines about behaviour (e.g. Christians believe we should follow The Ten Commandments, such as 'Thou shalt not kill'). Ask the children, either individually or in pairs, to brainstorm a list of basic rules which they think everyone should live by today.

Suggested activities

- Read 'My ten rules for today' (page 22). In groups, discuss Stefan's list of rules and compare them with the lists they have written. Ask each group to agree on their list of ten rules for today, then to share their views in a class discussion.

- Read 'A matter of conscience' (page 23). Ask pairs of students to discuss Terri's problem and decide what they would have done if they had been Terri.

- Invite individuals to complete the activity on Copymaster 5, which lists a number of different examples of antisocial behaviour and asks students to decide on their level of seriousness. Then ask groups to compare their views and to put the antisocial actions into a rank order.

Plenary

Ask groups to report their views on the seriousness of different antisocial actions and on how they ranked them. Discuss any major differences of opinion. Ask why they ranked some actions as more serious than others. Ask: "What would society be like if these antisocial activities were regarded as acceptable behaviour?" Point out that it is the responsible behaviour of the majority of people who avoid such antisocial actions that underpins society.

Extension activities

Role play the scene in which someone faces a similar situation to Terri's and has to make a decision based on their conscience about whether or not to join in with their friends.

Assessment

Use Copymaster 1A to assess students' learning by asking them to write their own guidelines, entitled 'Ten rules for today'. They must give a reason for each of their rules.

Your Life 1/Year 7

UNIT 5 You and your values – right and wrong

Lesson 2 *Your Life 1*, pages 24–25
National Curriculum Programme of Study for Citizenship coverage 1a, 2a, 2b, 2c; links with QCA exemplar unit 3

Objective: To examine the moral issue of whether it is right or wrong to tell on someone, and to discuss a number of situations involving a moral judgement.

Starter

Begin with a class discussion. Write the words 'informer', 'tell-tale', 'grass' and 'sneak' on the board. Ask: "Why do people despise anyone who tells tales? Are they right to do so?" "Does whether to tell depend on the circumstances, e.g. the seriousness of the incident?" "Is telling on someone who has attacked another person different from telling on someone who has stolen something?" "Does it make a difference if the person responsible is a relative or a friend?" "Does it make a difference if you've promised not to tell?" "Are there circumstances in which you should break such a promise?" End the discussion by emphasising that when faced with a difficult decision, each of us has to make up our mind about the right thing to do.

Suggested activities

- Read 'The right thing?' (page 24). In groups, discuss what the writer says about the difficulty of deciding when to tell or not to tell. Ask: "Which of his statements do you agree with?" "Which do you disagree with?" Invite students to share their own experiences of any dilemmas they have faced, but stress that they can choose whether or not to do so. Encourage them to share their views in a class discussion, and ask: "Do you think it often takes more courage to tell than not to tell?"

- Ask groups to discuss the ten situations described in the section 'What should you do if …?' (page 25). Point out that different people in the group may make different decisions and that the purpose of the activity is to help them to make up their own minds rather than to agree as a group.

Plenary

Ask the students to share their views on what to do in the ten situations. Talk about the pressure that a person can come under in difficult situations – sometimes from other children, sometimes from adults. Ask: "In such a situation, is there anyone you can turn to for advice or do you always have to rely on your own judgement?" "Can talking to a helpline or an independent adult, such as a counsellor, help?"

Extension activity

Ask the students to write their own essay entitled 'The right thing?' (see 'For your file' on page 25).

UNIT 5 You and your values – right and wrong

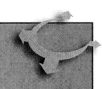

Your Life 1/Year 7

Lesson 3 *Your Life 1*, pages 26–27
National Curriculum Programme of Study for Citizenship coverage 1b, 2a, 2b, 2c

> **Objective:** To understand what manners are, and how, in a diverse society, people from different cultures have different customs which are important to respect.

Resources

Copies of Copymaster R4 'Developing as a citizen' (page 184)

Starter

Explain what manners are and draw two columns on the board, labelling one 'Good manners' and the other 'Bad manners'. Ask the students to suggest types of behaviour, which are considered good manners and bad manners, and list their suggestions under the columns on the board. Then ask: "Do you know of any behaviour that is regarded as good manners in our society, but considered bad manners in another society?" "Do you know of any behaviour that is regarded as good manners in another society, but bad manners in our society?" Discuss any examples the class can think of, then read the first paragraph on page 26.

Suggested activities

- Ask individuals to look at the ten statements about manners (page 26) and, for each statement, to decide whether they a) agree with the statement b) disagree with it or c) are not sure. Then invite them to share their views as a class.

- Read the information about table manners on page 27. Ask the students to work in groups to design the layout of either a leaflet or a page for a magazine for 10- to 11-year-olds on the subject of table manners. Encourage them to be creative. For example, in addition to text giving information, they could include cartoons and/or a comic strip or a story about a character called Billy Badmanners. Ask the groups to share their ideas in a class discussion.

Plenary

Ask the students to look again at the lists of good manners and bad manners, which they compiled at the start of the lesson. Add any other examples that have been discussed during the main activities. Focus on the list of bad manners. Ask: "Do you think some acts of bad manners are worse than others?" Focus on the list of good manners. Discuss why good manners are important.

Extension activities

Ask groups to produce their leaflet or magazine page on table manners.

Students interview a number of older people to find out their views on manners (see 'In pairs' page 26). Then ask individuals to write a statement saying how important they think good manners are (see 'For your file' page 26).

Ask students to choose a different society, e.g. Japanese society, and find out about manners in that society.

Recording and evaluating

Ask students to use the appropriate section of Copymaster R4 to help them to record and evaluate what they have learned from this unit.

Your Life 1/Year 7

UNIT 6 You and your family – getting on with others

Your Life 1/Year 7

Lesson 1 *Your Life 1*, pages 28–29
National Framework for PSHE coverage 3e, 3g, 3h, 3i

Objective: To explore the causes of tension between young people and their parents, and to understand that parents and children have different feelings and perspectives.

Starter

Ask the students to brainstorm the causes of arguments between them and their parents or carers. Then make a class list of the causes on the board. Tell them that the top five causes of arguments are: money, clothes, going out, helping at home and school. Explain that the aim of the lesson is to look at the causes of arguments and to discuss the different viewpoints that children and parents have.

Suggested activities

- In groups, ask students to read and discuss 'What causes arguments?' (page 29), before sharing their thoughts in a class discussion.

- Ask individuals to read 'Doing your share of the chores' (page 29), and to make a note of how often they help with each of the tasks. Then ask groups to compare how much they help and how much they think children should be expected to help.

- Study 'Problems with parents' (page 28). Read the article from *Shout* magazine and then, either in groups or as a class, discuss Laura's problem and the issue of parents giving their children enough privacy.

Plenary

Recap the main points that students made in the class discussion about quarrels over clothes and going out. Focus on the different viewpoints that parents and children have and why they are different. Try to encourage the class to agree on the ages at which children should be able to a) choose their own clothes, b) go out without telling their parents where they are going or c) decide the time they should come in. Then try to reach agreement on how much children should be expected to help adults with the chores.

Extension activities

Ask students to write their views on how much children should help with the household chores (see 'For your file' page 29).

Ask students to act out the role play (page 29), then hold a debrief in which they discuss their feelings and the alternative responses.

UNIT 6 You and your family – getting on with others

Your Life 1/Year 7

Lesson 2 *Your Life 1*, pages 30–31
National Framework for PSHE coverage 3e, 3g, 3h, 3i

Objective: To discuss ways of behaving that can help young people deal with difficulties in their relationships with parents, brothers and sisters.

Resources

Copies of Copymaster 6 'How to cope with brothers and sisters' (*Your Life 1 Copymasters*, page 18)

Copies of Copymaster R3 'Developing relationships' (page 183)

Starter

Recap the causes of arguments between young people and their parents discussed in the previous lesson. Ask: "What are the main causes of arguments between you and your brothers and sisters?" Explain that there are different ways of behaving when conflicts occur in families, and that the aim of the lesson is to discuss strategies for dealing with difficult situations.

Suggested activities

- Read the top ten tips on page 30. Ask the students to discuss the questions in groups, then to share their ideas in a class discussion.

- Read Annabel's problem and the advice she is offered (page 31). Ask groups to discuss her problem and decide what advice they would give her. Then read the poem 'Sisterly feelings' (page 31) and talk about feelings of jealousy and how to deal with them.

- Ask pairs or groups to draw up a list of tips on how to cope with their brothers and sisters, then to compare their list with the tips given on Copymaster 6. Ask: "Which of the tips from the two lists are the most helpful?"

Plenary

Write the words 'communication', 'consideration', 'co-operation' and 'compromise' on the board. Discuss what each word means and how they each suggest a way of behaving that can be useful in ensuring that the students maintain a good relationship with other members of their families.

Extension activities

Ask students to write a paragraph for their files to show their understanding of why following the four cs is a good way of behaving towards family members.

Ask pairs to develop role plays about arguments between brothers and/or sisters, showing different ways of reacting to the situation. Then hold a debrief in which they discuss their feelings and talk about the most constructive responses.

Ask pairs each to write a letter (either real or imaginary) to a magazine's agony aunt from someone who is having a problem with a brother or sister, then swap their letters and write the agony aunt's reply. Share the letters and replies in a group or class discussion.

Recording and evaluating

Ask students to fill in the appropriate section of Copymaster R3 to record and evaluate what they have learned from this lesson.

Your Life 1/Year 7

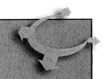

UNIT 7 You and your body – smoking

Your Life 1/Year 7

Lesson 1 *Your Life 1*, pages 32–33
National Framework for PSHE coverage 2b, 2d, 2g

Objective: To understand how smoking affects the health and appearance of people, and what the risks and the costs of smoking are.

Starter

Introduce the subject of smoking by asking students to say whether or not they are concerned about smoking ('I am/am not very concerned about smoking') and how high they think the risks from smoking are ('I think the risks from smoking are high/not very high'). Then explain that the lesson is going to examine how smoking affects people's health, the risks from smoking and the costs of smoking, and that you are going to ask them again about their attitudes to smoking at the end of the lesson to see whether they have changed their views.

Suggested activities

- Read 'Smoking – the facts' (page 32). Then ask the students to work in pairs to design a 'True or false' fact-check quiz about smoking. Help them to get started by giving them an example of a question: Less than 50% of lung cancer deaths are related to smoking. True or false? When they have finished, ask them to form groups of four and encourage each pair to do the other pair's quiz.

- Ask pairs to role play the scene (page 32) in which a non-smoker uses the information from 'Smoking – the facts' to try to persuade someone who has started smoking to give up.

- Read 'The high costs of smoking' (page 33) then ask the students, in groups, to script the three scenes suggested in the role-play activity on page 33.

Plenary

Ask students to think of three facts about smoking that they have learned from the lesson. Hold a class discussion in which they share the facts they have learned. Finally, ask them the same questions as you asked about attitudes to smoking at the beginning of the lesson. Have they changed their minds in any way as a result of what they have learned?

Extension activity

Ask students to demonstrate their understanding of smoking facts by designing a leaflet entitled 'Ten facts you should know about smoking'. They can use the internet to provide them with extra facts about smoking. Useful websites to look at include www.lifebytes.gov.uk.

Your Life 1/Year 7

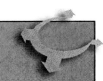

UNIT 7 You and your body – smoking

Your Life 1/Year 7

Lesson 2 *Your Life 1*, pages 34–35
National Framework for PSHE coverage 2b, 2d, 2g

Objective: To consider the reasons why people smoke, to examine the issue of passive smoking and to discuss the laws about tobacco.

Resources

Copies of Copymaster 7 'Smoking crossword' (*Your Life 1 Copymasters*, page 19)

Copies of Copymaster R2 'Keeping healthy' (page 182)

Starter

Draw two columns on the board. Label one 'Reasons for smoking' and the other 'Reasons for not smoking'. Hold a class discussion and write the reasons students suggest in the appropriate column. Then explain what is meant by passive smoking, and why the issue of passive smoking causes people to have strong views about where people should be allowed to smoke. Smokers argue that they have a right to smoke wherever they want, while non-smokers argue they should be able to avoid having to inhale other people's smoke.

Suggested activities

- Read 'What do you really think about smoking?' (page 34). Ask groups to discuss the questions on page 35 and to appoint someone to note down their views and then to report them in a class discussion.

- Read 'Tobacco and the law' (page 35). Ask groups to discuss the questions and to report their views in a class discussion.

- Talk about the situations in which a non-smoker might be pressurised by their friends to join them and have a cigarette. Then get them to act out the role play (page 35).

Plenary

Hold a debrief in which you discuss how hard it can be to say "No". Talk about strategies the students can use to be assertive (e.g. the 'broken record' strategy in which they simply keep repeating why they don't want to).

Extension activities

Ask students to complete the crossword (Copymaster 7) to demonstrate their knowledge and understanding of smoking.

Invite groups to investigate attitudes to smoking by carrying out a smoking survey. They can either design their own questionnaire or use the questionnaire in *Issues 1: Teacher's Resources* (Collins Educational). Ask them to analyse the completed questionnaires and to report their findings to the rest of the class.

Suggest individuals to write their own views on smoking issues in a letter to a magazine or newspaper.

Recording and evaluating

Ask students to fill in the appropriate section of Copymaster R2 to record and evaluate what they have learned from this unit.

UNIT 8 You and the law – children's rights

Your Life 1/Year 7

Lesson 1 *Your Life 1*, pages 36–37
National Curriculum Programme of Study for Citizenship coverage 1a, 1f, 2a, 2b, 2c; links with QCA exemplar units 1, 3

Objective: To explain what children's rights are at home and what parents' responsibilities are.

Resources

Copies of Copymaster 8 'Smacking – what do you think?' (*Your Life 1 Copymasters*, page 20)

Starter

Ask the students: "What is the difference between a right and a responsibility?" Write definitions and examples on the board: a right is something which you are entitled to, e.g. children have the right to be fed and clothed; a responsibility is something that you should do, e.g. parents have a responsibility to protect their children from harm.

Read the two paragraphs on 'Parents' duties and children's rights' (page 37). Discuss what is said about the responsibilities that parents have to care for their children and about what can happen if parents neglect their children or treat them cruelly.

Suggested activities

- Read 'Your rights at home' (page 37). Ask pairs to do the true/false quiz on page 36. Then hold a class discussion in which you give the answers: 1 True, 2 True, 3 False, 4 False, 5 True, 6 False, 7 False (but your views may be taken into account), 8 False (you have the right to go on seeing your dad, but in practice your mum may make it impossible for you to do so), 9 False, 10 False.

- Ask groups to discuss the statements on choice of schools, smacking and medical treatment on page 36. Then ask them to report their views in a class discussion.

Plenary

Summarise what the students have learned about parents' duties and children's rights by making lists on the board. You could then transfer the lists onto posters to display in the classroom. Explain that while society accepts that parents have responsibilities, they are not set out in law. Read the section on 'Parents' responsibilities – how the law works' (page 36). Discuss what parental responsibility means in law and how the law tries to put the interests of the child first.

Extension activity

Organise a class debate on the issue of smacking. Give out copies of Copymaster 8. Then split the class into four groups and ask two groups to prepare the arguments in support of smacking and two groups to prepare the arguments against smacking. Ask the groups to appoint a spokesperson to present their views. After the four representatives have given their speeches, invite contributions from the rest of the class. Then hold a vote to decide whether the class is for or against smacking. They can then write letters to a magazine giving their individual views.

UNIT 8 You and the law – children's rights

Your Life 1/Year 7

Lesson 2 *Your Life 1*, pages 38–39
National Curriculum Programme of Study for Citizenship coverage 1a, 1f, 2a, 2b, 2c; links with QCA exemplar units 1, 3

Objective: To examine the law regarding the ages at which children are allowed to do things, and the law concerning children being taken into care.

Resources

Copies of Copymaster 2A 'Understanding children's rights' (page 158)

Starter

Explain that the law in the UK aims to protect children by not allowing them to do certain things until they are considered old enough. Ask the students to write down the minimum ages at which they think the law allows them to a) open a bank account, b) buy a pet, c) go into a bar, d) buy an alcoholic drink, e) buy cigarettes, f) vote in local and parliamentary elections, g) drive a car, h) get married, i) choose their own doctor, j) join the armed forces.

Suggested activities

● Ask pairs to read 'Children and the law' (page 38) and to check whether or not the answers they wrote down were correct. Then, in groups, invite them to discuss the questions at the bottom of page 38, before holding a class discussion about what changes (if any) they think should be made to the law. Make a list on the board of the changes they suggest.

● Read 'Children in care' (page 39) and ask groups to discuss the questions. (Note: Be aware that there may be children in the group who are in care, and so the activity may need careful handling. In such circumstances, it may be better to hold a class discussion rather than group discussions.)

Plenary

Ask the students to write a short statement giving their views on the laws concerning children and whether any of them should be changed (see 'For your file' page 38). Remind them to refer to the list you wrote during the main activity to help them.

Extension activities

Suggest the students to interview a number of adults to find out their views on the laws concerning the ages at which children can do certain things. Hold a class discussion in which they report their findings. Do the adults' views differ from their views? If so, why do the students think this is?

Choose an issue on which the students feel very strongly that the age should be changed. Ask them to draft a letter to their local MP stating their arguments on why that particular law should be changed.

Assessment

Use copies of Copymaster 2A to assess understanding of children's rights. (Answers: All the statements are false with the exception of statement 7 and statement 10.)

Your Life 1/Year 7

UNIT 8 You and the law – children's rights

Your Life 1/Year 7

Lesson 3 *Your Life 1*, pages 40–41
National Curriculum Programme of Study for Citizenship coverage 1a, 1f, 2a, 2b, 2c, 3a; links with QCA exemplar units 3, 16

Objective: To explore what rights children have, to explain the laws concerning child employment in the UK and to examine child labour in the developing world.

Resources

Copies of Copymaster R4 'Developing as a citizen' (page 184)

Starter

Write up on the board: 'All children should be allowed to work whatever age they are'. Ask the students whether they agree or disagree with this statement. Ask: "Why aren't children allowed to work?" "Up to what age should children be prohibited from working?" "Should there be limits on the times when children can work and on the hours they work?" "What are the laws in the UK?" Read 'Child employment in Britain' (page 40) and discuss what the law is. Explain that the laws are designed to protect children, and that the aim of the lesson is to look at children's rights and at how child workers are exploited in many parts of the world.

Suggested activities

- Read 'The rights of the child' (page 40). Ask: "Do you think any of the rights are more important than others? Why?" "What other rights do children have?" Ask groups to draw up a charter of children's rights. Then hold a class discussion and, on the board, list the rights they agree all children have.

- Read 'Child labour in the developing world' (page 41). Discuss the different types of jobs done by children in the developing world, then read and discuss 'Sawai's story' (page 41). Talk with the class about how different Sawai's life is from theirs and how they would feel if they were in her position. Encourage them to imagine what it would be like to be a child labourer and to tell each other about a typical day in their life.

Plenary

Recap the list of rights, which the class agreed all children have. Refer to the charter of children's rights that you wrote on the board and ask them to copy it for their files.

Extension activities

Talk about organisations which exist to protect children's rights. Explain that the National Society for the Prevention of Cruelty to Children (NSPCC) works to protect children from abuse in the UK and that Anti-Slavery International campaigns throughout the world to stop children being forced to work for little or no money. Ask pairs to use the internet to research the work of the NSPCC (www.nspcc.org.uk) and Anti-Slavery International (www.anti-slavery.org). Ask them to make notes and to write a short report about how these organisations try to protect children's rights.

Recording and evaluating

Ask students to use the appropriate section of Copymaster R4 to help them to record and evaluate what they have learned from this unit.

UNIT 9 – You and other people – bullying

Your Life 1/Year 7

Lesson 1 *Your Life 1*, pages 42–43
National Framework for PSHE coverage 1b, 3a, 3j

> **Objective:** To explore what bullying is, to examine a case of bullying and to discuss who gets bullied.

Starter

Begin by setting ground rules for the discussion of the issue. Explain that the aim is to investigate bullying by looking at some examples, rather than by sharing personal experiences. Therefore, no one is allowed to talk about another person's experiences unless that person has first spoken about them, and no one has to talk about experiences in front of the class.

Ask: "What is bullying?" Invite students to brainstorm what they think bullying is and collect their ideas on the board. Then read the statements in 'What is bullying?' (page 42). Discuss the three questions that follow on page 42, either in groups or with the whole class. List on the board all the types of behaviour that they consider to be bullying and classify them according to whether they are physical, verbal or emotional bullying.

Suggested activities

- Read 'Jumble' (pages 42–43), then ask groups to do the discussion activity and to report their views in a class discussion. Ask them: "What would you have done if you had been the person who saw Barbara pull the coin out of her pocket? Would you have said something? Who would you have spoken to – Barbara or Lily?" "What would be the consequences of you speaking up or not speaking up?"

- Ask students to imagine that they are Lily and to say what Lily feels. Suggest they write an account of the afternoon's events from her point of view. Invite students to read out what they have written, and discuss what they have learned about bullying and its effects by identifying with Lily.

Plenary

Talk about why Lily is bullied. Explain that there is no such thing as a 'typical' victim, and read and discuss 'Who gets bullied?' (page 42). End by recapping the different types of bullying that they identified at the start of the lesson.

Extension activity

Do the role-play activity (page 43). Ask students to present their role plays to the rest of the class and discuss how it felt to be Lily. Which of the suggestions that Lily's sister makes in their role plays do they think would be the most helpful to Lily?

Your Life 1/Year 7

UNIT 9 – You and other people – bullying

Objective: To explain why people bully and what it feels like to be bullied.

Starter

Ask the students: "Why do some people bully others?" Encourage them to brainstorm their ideas and collect them on the board. Suggestions might include: "To have fun at the victim's expense", "To make themselves feel powerful", "Jealousy", "Spite", "Because they are racist". Explain that many bullies are people who have problems that they take out on others (e.g. they are insecure and unhappy, either at home or at school, and bullying is a way of giving themselves some status). Evidence suggests that people who bully have often been bullied themselves.

Suggested activities

- Read and discuss with the whole class the statements made by Tessa Sanderson and Martyn Lewis (page 44). Talk about why they were picked on and how it made them feel. Explain what prejudice means and how both of them were the victims of prejudice.

- Read 'Lana's story' (page 44) and 'Stephen's story' (page 45). Ask groups to discuss why they were bullied. Share the groups' views in a class discussion and ask: "How do these stories make you feel about bullying?"

- Read Prince Naseem Hassan's comments about bullying (page 44) and discuss them with the whole class. Do you agree or disagree with him? Is it harder and braver to walk away than to stand and fight?

- Read and discuss the poem 'It hurts' (page 45). Ask: "What is the message of the poem?" Ask students to do the writing activity (see 'For your file' page 45).

Plenary

Reread 'Stephen's story'. List the choices that Stephen has: to do nothing; to tell a teacher; to tell his parents; to talk to someone else; to ring a helpline. Ask students to imagine that they are the editor of a problem page and that Stephen has written to them – what would they say to him? Discuss their suggestions, before explaining that in the next lesson they will be exploring what to do if they are bullied.

Extension activities

Ask groups to perform the role play (page 45). Think carefully about the composition of the groups as you might want to keep certain children apart. Invite groups to present their role plays. Discuss how they show Stephen reacting and what they think is the best way for him to react.

In preparation for the next lesson, ask students to explore bullying issues on the internet. Information and advice on bullying can be found on these websites: The Anti-bullying Network (www.antibullying.net/youngadvice); ChildLine (www.childline.org.uk); Kidscape (www.kidscape.org.uk).

UNIT 9 – You and other people – bullying

Your Life 1/Year 7

Lesson 3 *Your Life 1*, pages 46–47
National Framework for PSHE coverage 1b, 3a, 3j

> **Objective:** To explore the different ways of reacting to bullying and to discuss what to do if you are being bullied.

Resources:

Copies of Copymaster 9 'The truth about bullying' (*Your Life 1 Copymasters*, page 21)

Copies of the school's policy on bullying

Copies of Copymaster R3 'Developing relationships' (page 183)

Starter

Write the words 'aggressive', 'assertive' and 'passive' on the board and explain what they mean. Talk about how the way you react to bullying may be aggressive, assertive or passive. Explain that the purpose of this lesson is to investigate the advantages and disadvantages of the different ways of reacting to bullying.

Suggested activities

- Ask pairs to study the eight situations described on page 46, to decide what they think is the best way of responding in each situation, then to share their views in a group discussion, followed by a class discussion. During the discussions, ask students to focus on the consequences of each type of action. Which action would help to defuse the situation? Which action would escalate the situation? Which action would be most likely to bring an end to the bullying? Which action would let the bullying continue?

- Read 'How to beat the bullies' (page 47). Ask pairs to identify what they consider to be the three most useful pieces of advice. Compare their views in a class discussion and focus on the importance of speaking out, reinforcing the views expressed in the article that it is not telling tales, and that everyone has a right to feel safe and happy.

- Read the advice given on 'Fogging' (page 47). Discuss what it is and how it works. Ask students to rank its value as a strategy on a scale of 1–10 (1 not very useful, 10 extremely useful) and to give reasons for their views.

Plenary

Draft a class bullying policy (see page 47). If copies of the school's bullying policy are available, as an alternative activity, they could study it critically, discuss how effective they think it is and suggest any alterations to make it more effective.

Extension activities

Study Copymaster 9. Ask students to compare the advice given in this article with the advice given on 'How to beat the bullies'. Which pieces of advice are the same? What other advice does this article give? Which do they find more useful?

Ask students to demonstrate their understanding of the issue of bullying by saying what they would plan to include in an article on bullying for a magazine, such as *Shout*, then to draft the article.

Recording and evaluating

Ask students to fill in the appropriate section of Copymaster R3 to record and evaluate what they have learned from this unit.

Your Life 1/Year 7

UNIT 10 You and the media – the power of television

Your Life 1/Year 7

Lesson 1 *Your Life 1*, pages 48–49
National Curriculum Programme of Study for Citizenship coverage 1h, 2a, 2b, 2c; links with QCA exemplar unit 9

Objective: To discuss the influence of television on people's lives and to examine whether it presents a fair and realistic picture of people and of life.

Resources

A video recording of an episode from a TV soap (optional – for extension activity only)

Starter

Ask the students: "How big an influence do you think television has on you?" "Do you think its influence is sometimes exaggerated?" Read 'Television and its influence' (page 48). Either in groups or as a class, discuss the six statements in turn. Conclude the discussion by asking for a show of hands: "Who thinks the influence of television is exaggerated?" "Do you think TV plays too big a part in your lives?"

Suggested activities

- Explain what a stereotype is (a standardised image of a type of person). Give an example of stereotyping, e.g. anyone with red hair has a quick temper. Then read 'TV isn't fair' (page 48) and discuss whether TV presents a fair picture of all sections of society. In addition to the questions on page 48, ask: "What sort of picture of teenagers does TV give?" "Is it a fair picture?"

- Introduce the topic of how realistic TV dramas are by asking students which soaps they watch. "Do you think that people actually behave like the characters in their favourite soaps?" Read 'Fact or fiction?' (page 49) and discuss what students learn about how realistic soaps are from a) the writer, b) the actress or c) the director.

Plenary

Invite students to write a short statement about the issues they have been discussing. Ask: "Do you think TV dramas give a picture of life as it really is?" "Do you think TV gives a fair representation of all sections of society?" "How much influence do you think TV has on your views and values?" Ask some of the students to read their statements to the rest of the class.

Extension activities

Organise a debate on the motion 'Television does more harm than good'. Begin by asking individuals to list what they consider to be the good points and the bad points about television. Then suggest they work in groups to draft speeches for the debate.

Show a video recording of an episode from a TV soap. Discuss it critically in the light of the comments from the writer, the actress and the director. Then ask students to do the writing task (see 'For your file' page 49).

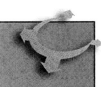

UNIT 10 You and the media – the power of television

Your Life 1/Year 7

Lesson 2 *Your Life 1*, pages 50–51
National Curriculum Programme of Study for Citizenship coverage 1h, 2a, 2b, 2c; links with QCA exemplar unit 9

Objective: To explore the issues of bias and viewpoints in TV programmes.

Resources

Copies of Copymaster 10 'One picture – two stories' (*Your Life 1 Copymasters*, page 22)

Copies of old newspapers/video recording of a TV news broadcast (optional – for extension activities only)

Copies of Copymaster 3A 'Understanding television' (page 159)

Copies of Copymaster R4 'Developing as a citizen' (page 184)

Starter

Write the words 'bias', 'objective' and 'subjective' on the board and explain their meanings. Discuss how we expect journalists to be unbiased and objective in their news reporting. Explain that, nevertheless, it is easy for a report to be biased, because of the viewpoint from which it is presented and through the language the reporter uses. Explain that the lesson is about bias in TV programmes.

Suggested activities

- Before studying the picture of the soldier (page 50), ensure that the students know who Saddam Hussein is and why the Americans and British remained in Iraq after the war to overthrow him. Draw attention to the use of emotive language ('tyrannical rule', 'invaded') which increases the bias. Then focus on the rainforest picture and discuss the bias in the two alternative commentaries.

- Hand out copies of Copymaster 10 and ask pairs to show their understanding of the different ways a picture can be viewed by preparing two alternative commentaries for each picture. Then ask them to present their pieces.

- Read 'The hero's point of view' (page 51). As a class, discuss what it says about seeing the action in dramas and sitcoms from a particular viewpoint. Discuss the final two paragraphs and what they say about news programmes.

Plenary

Read 'Viewpoint matters' (page 51). Ask: "What does it say about the effect of camera angles in news reports?" List on the board what people need to be aware of when watching TV news reports in order to detect bias.

Extension activities

Ask students to find pictures in old newspapers and to prepare two alternative commentaries on them. They could display them.

Watch a recording of a TV news broadcast. Discuss how the stories are presented.

Assessment

Use Copymaster 3A to assess students' understanding of television and its messages.

Recording and evaluating

Ask students to use the appropriate section of Copymaster R4 to help them to record and evaluate what they have learned from this lesson.

UNIT 11 You and your money – pocket money, budgeting and saving

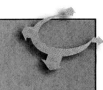

Your Life 1/Year 7

Lesson 1 *Your Life 1*, pages 52–53
National Framework for PSHE coverage 1g

> **Objective:** To discuss students' money-management skills by exploring how they handle their pocket money.

Starter

Write the words 'spendthrift' and 'miser' on the board and explain that a spendthrift is someone who spends money extravagantly, while a miser is someone who hoards their money. Ask the students to think about how they handle their money – are they a spender or a saver? Encourage them to rank themselves on a scale of 1–10 (1 = a spendthrift, 10 = a miser), and to explain to a friend why they gave themselves the ranking they did. Then explain to the class that you are going to ask them to complete a quiz and to see whether the results support their view of how they handle their money.

Suggested activities

- Ask the students to do the quiz on pages 52–53, taking time to think about each question and to answer honestly. Tell them to count up to see whether their answers are mostly **a**s, **b**s or **c**s, then to read the section 'What your answers say about how you handle your money'. Ask: "How does your self assessment compare with what the quiz says about how you handle your money?"

- Ask pairs to discuss their money-management skills and to suggest anything either of them needs to do in order to improve the way they handle their money.

Plenary

Read and discuss 'Money-management tips' (page 53). How helpful do students think the tips are? Can they suggest any other useful tips? Explain that the focus of the next lesson will be on pocket money problems and how to develop money-management skills by budgeting.

Extension activity

Ask students to research people's views on pocket money. Ask them to draw up a questionnaire aimed at either young people or parents and carers. Then encourage them to analyse the results and to present their findings in the form of a magazine article.

UNIT 11 You and your money – pocket money, budgeting and saving

Your Life 1/Year 7

Lesson 2 *Your Life 1*, pages 54–55
National Framework for PSHE coverage 1g

> **Objective:** To develop money-management skills by exploring pocket money issues and explaining how to work out a budget plan.

Resources

Copies of Copymaster 11 'The windfall' (*Your Life 1 Copymasters*, page 23)

Copies of Copymaster R1 'Understanding yourself' (page 181)

Starter

Introduce the topic by reading the first paragraph on page 54. Then ask pairs or groups to brainstorm the essentials they think parents or carers should provide, and the extras they think pocket money should be for (see 'What should your pocket money be for?', page 54). Draw two columns on the board and fill them in during a class discussion in which they share their ideas.

Suggested activities

- Ask groups to discuss the questions in 'What do you do with your pocket money?' (page 55). Ask them: "What conclusions can you draw from your discussions about how you spend your money?" "Do most of you spend it on the same things?" "Do most of you spend it all rather than save any of it?"

- Explain what a budget is and ask individuals to follow the steps in the flowchart in the section 'Planning a budget' (page 55). Challenge them to plan a budget for someone who will have a total of £15 available over the four weeks. Then ask them to discuss their budget plans in pairs. How would their plans be different if the person had £25 rather than £15?

- Ask pairs to read 'Pocket money problems' (page 54), then discuss the problems. Ask them what they would say in a letter to one of the children offering advice on how to deal with the problem. Share ideas in a class discussion.

Plenary

Ask the students to imagine they are planning an article on pocket money for a magazine for people of their own age. What would be their 'Top tips on how to handle your cash'? Hold a class discussion and list their ideas on the board.

Extension activities

Ask pairs to role play the scene 'I've spent my school trip money' (page 55). Invite some of them to perform their role plays and discuss what they suggest the person should do.

Give out copies of Copymaster 11. Ask groups to discuss the questions, then share their views in a class discussion. Invite the students to demonstrate their understanding of how to save money by preparing a reply to someone who has written asking for advice on how to save £100.

Recording and evaluating

Ask students to fill in the appropriate section of Copymaster R1 to record and evaluate what they have learned from this unit.

Your Life 1/Year 7

UNIT 12 You and your body – drugs and drugtaking

Your Life 1/Year 7

Lesson 1 *Your Life 1*, pages 56–57
National Framework for PSHE coverage 2d

Objective: To consider why some drugs are socially acceptable and others illegal, to discuss what drug abuse is and to understand the effects illegal drugs have.

Resources

Copies of Copymaster 12 'The language of drugs' (*Your Life 1 Copymasters*, page 24)

Starter

Introduce the topic by explaining that when we talk about drugs we often mean illegal drugs, but that there are other kinds of drugs. What other kinds of drugs can the students think of? Talk about drugs which are medicinal and drugs which are socially acceptable. Read and discuss 'What do we mean by 'drugs'?' (page 56). Discuss the view that if alcohol and tobacco had only recently been discovered, they would be banned (see 'In pairs' page 56).

Suggested activities

- Read the two statements in 'What is drug abuse?' (page 56). Ask groups to draft their own definitions of drug abuse, then compare them in a class discussion.

- Ask groups to read the information on 'How drugs can affect you' and 'Drugs can kill' on page 57. Invite them to show their understanding of the effects drugs can have by preparing a list of 'Ten ways drugs can affect your life'. Then ask individuals to write a statement saying how dangerous they think drugtaking is.

Plenary

Ask the students: "Do you think the dangers of drugtaking are exaggerated?" "Why are adults so concerned about drugtaking?" Ask individuals to read their statements about how dangerous they think drugtaking is, and discuss their views.

Extension activities

Ask students to design a poster to warn people of their age about the dangers of drugtaking.

Encourage them to demonstrate their knowledge and understanding of the terms used when discussing drugs and drugtaking by completing the matching exercise on Copymaster 12.

Your Life 1/Year 7

UNIT 12 You and your body – drugs and drugtaking

Your Life 1/Year 7

Lesson 2 *Your Life 1*, pages 58–59
National Framework for PSHE coverage 2d

Objective: To explore why people start to take drugs and to discuss attitudes towards drugs and drugtaking.

Resources

Copies of Copymaster R2 'Keeping healthy' (page 182)

Starter

Recap what the students learned about the effects drugs can have on a person's life (see Lesson 1). Explain that although people are aware of the dangers, some people take drugs. Explain that a focus for this lesson is on *why* they start to take drugs. Read the extract from *Drugs* by Anita Naik on page 58 and make the point that there isn't one single reason why people take drugs.

Suggested activities

- Ask students to read the statements on page 58 alone, and to rank the reasons given in the box at the foot of the page in order, starting with what they consider to be the main reason. Tell them to include any other reasons that they can suggest. Point out, however, that the focus is on the recreational use of drugs and that sports people taking drugs to enhance their performance is a separate issue. Invite students to share their views in a group discussion and to produce a group statement to share with the rest of the class.

- Read 'I'm really worried about my brother' (page 59), and ask groups to discuss the advice that is given and the question of what you should do if you discover that your brother or sister is taking drugs.

Plenary

Read Sammy's statement 'People are pressurised into drugs' (page 59). As a class, discuss the points she makes and why they agree or disagree with them.

Extension activities

- Ask students to complete the writing activity (see 'For your file' page 59), explaining their attitude towards drugs and drugtaking. Then organise a drugs forum in which you chair a discussion of the issues raised in the lesson. Ask individuals to form a panel and to start the debate by reading out what they have written.

- Suggest students use the internet to research information about, and attitudes towards, drugs and drugtaking. For information on the subject for 11- to 14-year-olds, see www.lifebytes.gov.uk.

Recording and evaluating

Ask students to fill in the appropriate section of Copymaster R2 to record and evaluate what they have learned from this unit.

Your Life 1/Year 7

UNIT 13 You and the community – being a good neighbour

Your Life 1/Year 7

Lesson 1 *Your Life 1*, pages 60, 62
National Curriculum Programme of study for Citizenship coverage 1g, 2a, 2b, 2c, 3a; links with QCA exemplar units 1, 4, 13

Objective: To explore what being a good neighbour involves and to examine the problem of vandalism.

Resources

Copies of Copymaster 13 'How good a neighbour are you?' (*Your Life 1 Copymasters*, page 25)

Copies of Copymaster 4A 'Understanding what being a good neighbour means' (page 160)

Starter

Explain that as a neighbour you have responsibilities as well as rights. Ask: "What makes a good neighbour?" Prompt pairs to brainstorm their definition of a good neighbour. Then ask groups to compare their definitions, to discuss the comments on page 60 and to draft a group statement about what makes a good neighbour to share with the rest of the class.

Suggested activities

- Ask pairs of students to discuss their ideas on how to be a good neighbour. Then invite them to compare their ideas with Hassan and Philip's list, to do the ranking activity (see 'How to be a good neighbour', page 60), and to discuss their views in groups.

- Suggest the students complete the quiz on Copymaster 13, then compare their answers in a group discussion.

- Explain what antisocial behaviour is and how vandalism is just one form of antisocial behaviour. Read 'Vandalism – a costly problem' (page 62). Ask students to discuss the four questions in groups, then to share their views in a class discussion.

Plenary

Discuss what the students have learned from the lesson about their rights and responsibilities as neighbours, and compile lists on the board.

Extension activities

Ask students to write a short statement for their files to show their understanding of what rights they have as a neighbour and what responsibilities they have.

Read 'Donna's story' (page 62). Ask groups to discuss how serious they think graffiti writing is and what they think Donna should have done. They can then work individually to write their views on graffiti writing.

Ask students to either write a story about an act of vandalism which leads to someone getting hurt or to design a poster about vandalism, pointing out how dangerous and costly it is (see 'For your file', page 62).

Ask your Community PC to come into school and talk to the students.

Assessment

Use Copymaster 4A to assess students' understanding of what being a good neighbour involves.

UNIT 13 You and the community – being a good neighbour

Your Life 1/Year 7

Lesson 2 *Your Life 1*, pages 61, 63
National Curriculum Programme of Study for Citizenship coverage 1c, 2a, 2b, 2c, 3a, 3b; links with QCA exemplar unit 1

Objective: To discuss how the neighbourhood might be improved and to explore how to take community action to improve it.

Resources

Copies of Copymaster R4 'Developing as a citizen' (page 184)

Starter

Remind the students that one of the points you identified in the previous lesson about being a good neighbour is to take care of the environment. Explain that this means not only avoiding antisocial behaviour, such as dropping litter or vandalism, but also taking steps to try to improve the neighbourhood.

Explain what an assessment is and how, in order to help them identify what needs to be done in the neighbourhood, they will start by assessing existing facilities and services and the current state of the environment.

Suggested activities

- Ask groups to carry out the discussion activities on 'Facilities and services', 'Safety' and 'Appearance' (page 61). Write the headings 'Facilities and services', 'Safety' and 'Appearance' on the board and, during a class discussion of their ideas, make lists of their suggestions for improvements.

- Read the newspaper article 'Pupils put on a show at the palace' (page 63). Then invite students to discuss the questions in groups, before holding a class discussion in which they share any further ideas. Add any new suggestions under the appropriate heading.

Plenary

Explain that identifying what you think needs to be done is only the first step. Next you need to check that it is what people want. Read and explain the various steps involved in developing a community action project (see the flowchart on page 63). Discuss how to tackle the next step – drafting a questionnaire.

Extension activities

Ask groups to follow the steps in the flowchart, beginning with drafting a questionnaire and carrying out the survey. After they have analysed the survey, students can either draft an action plan as suggested or, alternatively, write a report of their findings for the local newspaper.

Suggest students research how to set up or join a youth action group to try to improve their neighbourhood by visiting the National Youth Agency website: www.nya.org.uk.

Recording and evaluating

Ask students to use the appropriate section of Copymaster R4 to help them to record and evaluate what they have learned from this unit.

Your Life 1/Year 7

UNIT 14 You and your opinions – how to express your ideas

Your Life 1/Year 7

Lesson 1 *Your Life 1*, pages 64–65
National Curriculum Programme of Study for Citizenship coverage 2a, 2b, 2c; links with QCA exemplar unit 5

Objective: To develop the communication skills that will enable students to express their opinions effectively in exploratory group discussions.

Starter

Introduce the topic by asking: "What is the purpose of group discussions?" Collect the students' ideas on the board, then read the introductory section on page 64 and explain the aim of the lesson.

Suggested activities

- Ask students: "How do you organise a good group discussion?" "What guidelines can you follow to make sure that you have a successful discussion?" Read the guidelines 'Taking part' (page 64) and discuss them with the whole class.

- Explain that it is important always to appoint a chairperson to organise and control the discussion. Read and discuss the role of the chair in 'Chairing the discussion' (page 64). Explain that it is important also to appoint a secretary/reporter to write down the main points people make, so that they can then be reported in a class discussion.

- Read the articles about animals in circuses ('Are circuses degrading?' page 65), then encourage groups to discuss their opinions about circus animals and to report their views in a class discussion.

Plenary

Ask students to reflect on the process of taking part in group discussions by inviting at least one member of each group to say how successful or unsuccessful their group discussion was, explaining the reasons why.

Extension activity

Ask students to perform the role-play activity (page 65). Choose four students to be members of the panel, then split the class into four groups and ask them to assist the panel members in preparing their different views. Either act as the presenter yourself or choose a student who will perform the role effectively.

UNIT 14 You and your opinions – how to express your ideas

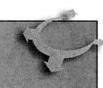

Your Life 1/Year 7

Lesson 2 *Your Life 1*, page 66
National Curriculum Programme of Study for Citizenship coverage 2a, 2b, 2c

Objective: To develop their ability to prepare a speech, expressing and justifying an opinion.

Resources

Copies of Copymaster 14 'Shooting and fishing – what do you think?' (*Your Life 1 Copymasters,* page 26)

Starter

Explain that when you are asked to give a speech expressing an opinion, you have to do three things: 1) research the issue, 2) prepare the speech and 3) deliver the speech. Talk about how you can research the topic (see 'Helpful hint' page 66) and how it is important to identify the arguments for and against a topic, so as to be able to argue an opinion effectively.

Suggested activities

- Read 'Preparing your speech' (page 66) and ask groups to add other arguments for and against boxing to Tony's list 'Boxing should be banned'. Then invite them to draw up their own lists for and against blood sports.

- Read 'Planning your speech' and discuss how Prisha used a flowchart to plan her speech. Draw attention to the structure of her speech: an introductory paragraph, followed by three paragraphs stating her arguments against zoos, then two paragraphs saying why the arguments for zoos are flawed, and a final paragraph in which she sums up her viewpoint.

- Ask students to use the rest of the lesson to plan a speech expressing their opinion on an animal rights topic such as zoos or circuses. You could distribute copies of Copymaster 14 for them to read the articles and to plan a speech expressing their views on shooting and fishing.

Plenary

Conclude the lesson by getting students to share the flowcharts they drew up while planning their speeches.

Your Life 1/Year 7

UNIT 14 You and your opinions – how to express your ideas

Your Life 1/Year 7

Lesson 3 *Your Life 1*, page 67
National Curriculum Programme of Study for Citizenship coverage 2a, 2b, 2c

Objective: To understand how to deliver a speech effectively.

Resources

Copies of Copymaster 5A 'Assessing your speaking skills' (page 161)

Starter

Read page 67 and discuss the list of points to remember when delivering a speech.

Suggested activity

- Ask some of the class to deliver their speeches. Invite the rest of the class to use the list of points to assess their delivery, giving marks out of ten. Stress that the aim of the assessment is firstly to give the speaker credit for what they did well, then to point out the things they could work to improve on next time they give a speech.

Plenary

Ask the students to discuss what they have learned from the lesson about how to deliver a speech effectively.

Extension activity

Organise a class debate. Either ask the class to choose their own topic and draft their own motion, or suggest a motion such as 'This house believes that boxing should be banned'. Choose four main speakers (a proposer and seconder, and an opposer and seconder). Help them to prepare their speeches. Open the debate with the proposer and their seconder, followed by the opposer and their seconder, then invite contributions from the rest of the class, before taking a vote.

Assessment

Use Copymaster 5A to assess their speaking skills.

UNIT 14 You and your opinions – how to express your ideas

Your Life 1/Year 7

Lesson 4 *Your Life 1*, pages 68–69
National Curriculum Programme of Study for Citizenship coverage 2a, 2b

Objective: To develop their ability to express and justify their opinions in writing.

Resources

Copies of Copymaster R4 'Developing as a citizen' (page 184)

Starter

Write the words 'purpose' and 'audience' on the board. Discuss how when you are writing to express an opinion your purpose is to persuade and how you structure and organise your writing will depend to a certain extent on your audience. Talk about how the audience will also affect your style and the language you use. For example, a letter to a friend will be more informal than a letter to a magazine, and an article for an adult audience may be written in different language to one for a teenage magazine.

Suggested activities

● Read the four letters in the section 'In my opinion' (page 68), then allow groups time to discuss which one they think should win the prize as Letter of the Week. Share the reasons for their choice in a class discussion. Then ask them to work individually to write a reply to one of the letters (see 'For your file' page 68).

● Read and discuss with the class the advice given in the flowchart on how to write an article or essay (page 69). Discuss Dominic's plan for an article on Bonfire Night, drawing attention to how he has an introductory statement, followed by a separate paragraph for each point of his argument, and a final paragraph summing up his opinion. Then ask the students, in pairs, to draw up a flowchart for an article, giving their opinion on whether parents should be allowed to smack their children.

Plenary

Recap the step-by-step guidelines on how to write an article or essay and ask students to make a copy of the flowchart for their file.

Extension activity

Ask individuals to write an article for a newspaper for young people, either on a subject on which they hold a strong opinion or on one of the topics suggested in 'For your file' (page 69).

Recording and evaluating

Ask students to use the appropriate section of Copymaster R4 to help them to record and evaluate what they have learned from this unit.

Your Life 1/Year 7

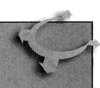

UNIT 15 You and your body – eating and exercise

Lesson 1 *Your Life 1*, pages 70–71
National Framework for PSHE coverage 2b, 2f

> **Objective:** To understand what a healthy diet is and why it is important to eat a balanced diet.

Starter

Talk about how if we eat too little food we may become ill through undernourishment, and how if we eat too much food we can become overweight. Define 'obesity' (being extremely overweight) and explain how it is linked with eating too much fat and sugar, and how it can lead to health problems, such as heart disease and diabetes. Define 'a balanced diet' (eating the right amounts of a variety of different foods) and that the aim of the lesson is to discuss what constitutes a healthy diet.

Suggested activities

- Read 'Healthy eating facts' (page 70) and discuss, first in groups and then as a class, what it says about the different foods your body needs. Draw attention to the fact that many people eat too much fat, sugar and salt, and point out that many junk foods contain high amounts of these.

- Ask groups to read and discuss 'What's for lunch?' (page 70). Then, as a class, discuss why Francesca's lunch is the healthiest, followed by Lauren's, with Sam and Darren having the least healthy meals. Ask groups to compare how healthy their own lunches are.

- Ask groups to read and discuss 'Trudy's eating diary' (page 71) and to report their views in a class discussion (see 'In pairs'). Plus points they should make include: she has three good meals a day at weekends; her lunches and suppers always include foods containing protein. Minus points include: she doesn't always have breakfast on schooldays; she needs to eat more fruit as she doesn't like vegetables; she needs to think about eating healthier snacks as cakes and biscuits are full of sugar and crisps contain too much salt.

Plenary

Read 'Healthy eating tips' (page 71) and discuss with the class the reason for each piece of advice. List on the board any further suggested tips.

Extension activities

Ask students to demonstrate their understanding of healthy eating by designing a leaflet offering advice to other students on what they should eat in order to have a healthy lunch.

Ask students to keep a food diary similar to 'Trudy's eating diary' and to rate their diet on a scale of 1–10 (1 = very unhealthy, 10 = very healthy). Discuss in groups how healthy they think their diet is and what they could do to improve it.

Involve students in the Britain On The Move campaign (www.britainonthemove.com).

UNIT 15 You and your body – eating and exercise

Your Life 1/Year 7

Lesson 2 *Your Life 1*, pages 72–73
National Framework for PSHE coverage 2b, 2c, 2f

Objective: To understand the importance of exercise to a healthy lifestyle and of developing a healthy attitude to your body shape.

Resources

Copies of Copymaster 15 'How healthy are you?' (*Your Life 1 Copymasters*, page 27)

Copies of Copymaster R2 'Keeping healthy' (page 182)

Starter

Introduce the topic by asking: "Why is it a good idea to exercise?" List the reasons the students suggest on the board, e.g. it's fun; it helps you to relax; it keeps you fit; it stops you getting fat; it's a good way of meeting people and making friends. Then read the introductory paragraph on page 72.

Suggested activities

- Read 'Some good reasons for taking exercise' (page 72) and discuss the various ways that exercise helps to keep your body in good condition. Then ask students to show their understanding of the value of exercise by preparing a reply from a magazine's agony aunt to a letter from Sam, a self-confessed couch potato who thinks exercise a waste of time, explaining to her why she should take exercise regularly. **A0**

- Read the first three paragraphs on page 73 about body shape and discuss the factors which determine it, explaining what is meant by the term 'metabolic rate'.

- Read 'Losing weight' (page 73) and talk about the pressures to conform to acertain shape. Discuss whether boys are under as much pressure as girls and, if not, why there is more pressure on girls.

Plenary

Read and discuss the advice given in the article 'Going on a diet' (page 73). Then recap what eating a balanced diet means and repeat the reasons why it is important to get enough exercise.

Extension activities

Challenge individuals to complete the quiz 'How healthy are you?' on Copymaster 15. Then ask them to write a comment saying what their answers tell them about how healthy their diet is and whether they are taking enough exercise.

Ask individuals to keep an exercise diary for a week, and then to set themselves a realistic target for getting themselves fitter if they discover that they need to do so (see 'In pairs', page 72).

Organise a debate either on the motion: 'This house believes that exercise is a waste of time' or 'This house believes there should be twenty minutes compulsory PE every school day.'

Recording and evaluating

Ask students to fill in the appropriate section of Copymaster R2 to record and evaluate what they learned from this unit.

Your Life 1/Year 7

UNIT 16 You as a citizen – Britain's government

Your Life 1/Year 7

Lesson 1 *Your Life 1*, page 74
National Curriculum Programme of Study for Citizenship coverage 1a; links with QCA exemplar units 1, 3

> **Objective:** To understand why we have laws, that different countries have different laws, and the distinction between criminal law and civil law.

Starter

Hold a class discussion on the question 'Why do we have laws?' Write the reasons the students suggest on the board. Discuss how different countries have different laws, and how laws not only protect your rights but also define your responsibilities. Read the section 'The law of the land' (page 74).

Suggested activities

- Ask groups to discuss what rules they would make for a group of people shipwrecked on a desert island.

- Invite each group to list their rules on a large sheet of paper and to appoint a spokesperson to explain the reasons for their rules in a class discussion.

- Encourage the class to agree on a set of rules, based on the suggestions made by the groups.

- Discuss the rights that each rule protects and the responsibilities each rule puts on every member of the shipwrecked group.

Plenary

Focus on 'Laws and law courts' (page 74). Make sure that the students understand the difference between criminal law and civil law. Discuss the types of cases that are dealt with in civil courts, e.g. family disputes such as divorce and custody cases, financial and property disputes, contract cases and cases involving libel and slander.

Extension activities

Ask students to write an article for a magazine aimed at Year 6 children, explaining why we have laws and what this means in terms of our rights and responsibilities.

Explain that in some countries the law of the land can be used to take away people's rights rather than to protect them. For example, a dictator may pass a law that denies people the right to free speech, making it an offence to criticise the government. In a democracy such as Britain, a law may be passed which affects your human rights. Suggest students use the internet to research the views of the human rights organisation Liberty and to find out its concerns about existing laws and proposed new laws, e.g. the introduction of identity cards (www.liberty-human-rights.org.uk).

UNIT 16 You as a citizen – Britain's government

Your Life 1/Year 7

Lesson 2 *Your Life 1*, pages 75–77
National Curriculum Programme of Study for Citizenship coverage 1c, 1d, 2a, 2b, 2c; links with QCA exemplar unit 6

Objective: To understand what Parliament is and what it does.

Resources

A short video-recording of TV coverage of Parliament, e.g. Prime Minister's Question Time

Starter

Ask the students: "What is Parliament?" Draw out the points made in the first paragraph on page 75.

Ask: "What does Parliament do?" Make a list of their suggestions on the board. Compare their list with the list on page 75.

Suggested activities

- Read 'Who runs Parliament?' (page 75). Discuss where the power lies today.

- Explain what is meant by 'devolution'. Ask groups to read the section 'Regional government' and to discuss what they learn from it about the powers of the various regional bodies.

- Show the video of Parliament at work and discuss with the class what they learn from it about what happens in the House of Commons. Then ask the students to study the information on their own on page 76 and to carry out the note-making activity (see 'For your file').

- Read the information about the House of Lords on page 77. Either ask groups to discuss the views on House of Lords reform and then to report back their opinions, or hold a whole class discussion followed by a vote on whether they think the House of Lords should be replaced by an elected assembly. Students can then write a letter to a newspaper explaining their opinion and the reasons for it.

Plenary

Recap what Parliament is and what it does, stressing the differences in the membership and roles of the House of Commons and the House of Lords.

Extension activities

Students can find out more about Parliament and what it does from the Parliamentary Education website 'Explore Parliament' (www.3T.co.uk/parliament).

Your Life 1/Year 7

UNIT 16 You as a citizen – Britain's government

Your Life 1/Year 7

Lesson 3 *Your Life 1*, pages 78–79
National Curriculum Programme of Study for Citizenship coverage 1c, 1d, 2a, 2b; links with QCA exemplar unit 6

> **Objective:** To understand what the government and the opposition are, and how the government is financed.

Starter

Discuss what a political party is and what the main political parties are. Read 'What are political parties?' (page 78) and explain that after an election the leader of the political party which has the most votes forms the government.

Suggested activities

- Read the information about the government, the cabinet and the opposition (page 78). Discuss what other ministers are members of the cabinet, e.g. Minister of Defence, Minister of Education. Start to compile a 'Who's who in Parliament'. If students are unsure who holds a particular post, ask them to check, using the internet.

- Ask individuals to study 'The finances of government' (page 79) and to make notes for their files under the headings: 'How the government raises money'; 'How the government spends money'; and 'How the government's finances are controlled'.

- Invite students to show their understanding of parliamentary terms by compiling a glossary from the information on pages 75–79.

AO

Plenary

Recap with the class what they have learned during the lesson about how the government is organised, what the opposition is and about the government's finances.

Extension activity

Create a newsboard about the government in action by getting the students to cut out newspaper articles on current political issues and displaying them on the classroom noticeboard.

Your Life 1/Year 7

UNIT 16 You as a citizen – Britain's government

Your Life 1/Year 7

Lesson 4 *Your Life 1*, pages 80–81
National Curriculum Programme of Study for Citizenship coverage 1d, 1e, 2a, 2b, 2c; links with QCA exemplar units 6, 12

Objective: To understand the electoral system and to compare different voting systems.

Resources

Copies of Copymaster 16 'The electoral system: a class debate' (*Your Life 1 Copymasters*, page 28)

Copies of Copymaster 6A 'Understanding Parliament and Parliamentary elections' (page 162)

Copies of Copymaster R4 'Developing as a citizen' (page 184)

Starter

Write the word 'democracy' on the board. Explain that it means a system of government where all the citizens share power. Talk about how it would be impossible for everyone in the UK to meet in order to make decisions, so we delegate power to elected representatives in a decision-making body – Parliament.

Suggested activities

- Read and discuss 'How MPs are elected' on page 80. Then ask pairs to compile a 'True or false?' quiz about elections. Then swap their quiz with another pair's.

- Explain that fewer than 6 out of 10 people voted in the 2001 general election. Ask: "Why do you think people didn't vote?" "What can be done to encourage people to vote?" e.g. hold the vote on Sundays; introduce electronic voting and/or postal voting; put polling booths in supermarkets; make voting compulsory. Make a list of suggestions on the board.

- Read and discuss the information on page 81, explaining the differences between 'first past the post' voting system and proportional representation systems. Hold a class discussion on voting systems (see 'In groups' page 81).

Plenary

Divide the class into two teams and recap what they have learned about elections by asking them questions based on the information on these pages (e.g. How often must a general election be held? How old must you be to vote?). If one team fails to answer correctly, offer the question to the other team for a bonus point.

Extension activities

Read and discuss the arguments presented on Copymaster 16. Then hold a formal debate on the motion: 'This house believes that the British electoral system is unfair and that proportional representation should be introduced.'

Assessment

Use Copymaster 6A to assess understanding of Parliament and parliamentary elections. Answers: 1) c, 2) c, 3) a, 4) b, 5) c, 6) c, 7) b, 8) b, 9) c, 10) c, 11) b, 12) a, 13) b, 14) c, 15) c.

Recording and evaluating

Ask students to use the appropriate section of Copymaster R4 to help them to record and evaluate what they learned from this unit.

Your Life 1/Year 7

UNIT 17 You and the community – taking action: raising money for a charity

Your Life 1/Year 7

Lesson 1 *Your Life 1*, pages 82–83
National Curriculum Programme of Study for Citizenship coverage 1f, 2a, 3b; links with QCA exemplar unit 1

Objective: To discuss raising money for a charity and to decide from a group of charities which one to support.

Resources

Leaflets produced by the charities which they are considering (optional)

Starter

Read out this statement: 'I know I should give money to charity, but I hate it when I see a charity collection in the street and feel guilty if I don't give anything'. Ask: "What's your view of giving money to charity?" Invite students to share their views in a class discussion.

Suggested activity

- Ask groups to read the information about the ten different charities on page 82–83 (together with any leaflets that you have been able to obtain from the charities) in order to decide on which two charities they recommend should be supported. Write on the board a list of points for them to consider:

  Do you want to support a charity which helps –

  animals or people?

  people in the UK or in developing countries?

  conservation of the environment?

  people with disabilities?

  the homeless?

  people whose lives are in danger?

- Invite students to prepare a statement giving their first and second choices of charity, using the description of what the charity does to help support their decision. Then share their views in a class discussion before voting on which two charities they would choose to support.

Plenary

Discuss together the reasons why students rejected some charities and preferred others. How difficult was it for them to choose? What were the particular reasons for choosing the two charities they decided to support?

Extension activity

Ask students to imagine that someone has offered to donate £25 to one of the ten charities described on these pages. Suggest students write a letter to the person, explaining which of the charities they think they should support and why.

UNIT 17 You and the community – taking action: raising money for a charity

Your Life 1/Year 7

Lesson 2 *Your Life 1*, pages 84–85
National Curriculum Programme of Study for Citizenship coverage 1f, 2a, 3b;
links with QCA exemplar unit 1

Objective: To choose a local charity to support, to decide on and plan a fund-raising activity.

Resources

Copies of Copymaster 17 'How to hold a committee meeting' (*Your Life 1 Copymasters*, page 29)

Copies of Copymaster 7A 'Understanding your values' (page 163)

Copies of Copymaster R4 'Developing as a citizen' (page 184)

Starter

Introduce the idea of raising money for a local charity by asking for suggestions of local charities the students might support. Read the two introductory paragraphs on page 84, then make a list of suggested charities on the board. Be prepared to prompt, if necessary, by making a list of possible charities prior to the lesson.

Suggested activities

- Ask groups to discuss the list of local charities and to choose one which they would like to support. Invite them to share their views in a class discussion.

- Study the 'Fund-raising activities' on page 84. Can the class suggest any others? Add them to the list, then have a class discussion and hold a vote to choose one.

- Read 'Organising a fund-raising event' on page 85 and discuss which jobs the class decided needed doing when organising a second-hand sale. Talk about the groups they set up and what the responsibilities of each group were. Ask the class to make a similar list of jobs that need to be done for their planned event and to list in detail the responsibilities of the group in charge of each job.

Plenary

Discuss the steps you would need to take in order actually to organise the event. Introduce the idea of setting up a planning committee (see 'The planning committee' on page 85). Discuss together whether or not it is practicable to organise the events and make a decision on whether or not you are going to go ahead.

Extension activities

Read and discuss Copymaster 17. Discuss the responsibilities of a) the chairperson, b) the secretary and c) all the committee members. Then ask groups to draw up an agenda for the meeting of a planning committee organising either the event the class chose or a sale of second-hand books and toys.

Plan and hold your fund-raising event for a local charity. For advice contact The Giving Campaign (www.givingcampaign.org.uk).

Assessment

Use Copymaster 7A to assess understanding of organising a fund-raising event.

Recording and evaluating

Ask students to use the appropriate section of Copymaster R4 to record and evaluate what they have learned from this unit.

Your Life KS3 Co-ordinator's File © HarperCollinsPublishers Ltd 2005. This page may be photocopied for use in the classroom.

UNIT 18 You and other people – people with disabilities

Your Life 1/Year 7

Lesson 1 *Your Life 1*, pages 86–87
National Framework for PSHE coverage 3a, 3b; National Curriculum
Programme of Study for Citizenship coverage 3a; links with QCA exemplar
unit 1

Objective: To understand what is meant by disability, to explain how people become disabled and to explore what it is like to have a disability.

Resources

Copies of Copymaster 18 'Becoming disabled' (*Your Life 1 Copymasters*, page 30)

Starter

Ask the students: "What do you understand by the term 'disability'?" Read 'Defining disability' (page 86) and discuss the difference between the two definitions. Then read 'What is a disability?' (page 86) and explain the point it makes about how physical and social barriers disable a person with an impairment from participating fully in the community.

Suggested activities

- Read 'Becoming disabled' (page 86) and discuss the various ways that impairments occur. Read and discuss the information on Copymaster 18 about the most common medical conditions which cause an impairment. Invite pairs to show their understanding of the information by compiling a quiz, then to swap their quiz with another pair.

- Read 'What is it like to have a disability?' (page 87). Discuss in groups, then as a class, what they learn from the statements about how people with a disability feel about the attitudes of able-bodied people towards them.

Plenary

Read 'A way with words' (page 87) and discuss how the language people use when discussing disabilities can be negative and discriminate by stereotyping people. Recap what the students have learned about what it is like to have a disability. Emphasise that people with disabilities want the able-bodied to recognise them as individuals and as people, rather than to stereotype them or pity them because of their impairment.

Extension activity

Invite individuals or pairs to use the internet to research one of the medical conditions which can cause an impairment. They can then either produce a fact sheet on it or prepare a short talk about it to give to the rest of the class.

UNIT 18 You and other people – people with disabilities

Your Life 1/Year 7

Lesson 2 *Your Life 1*, pages 88–89
National Framework for PSHE coverage 3a, 3b; National Curriculum Programme of Study for Citizenship coverage 3a; links with QCA exemplar unit 1

Objective: To understand the needs of people with disabilities and to challenge the stereotyped view of people with disabilities.

Resources

Copies of Copymaster R3 'Developing relationships' (page 183)

Starter

Ask the students to consider the following: "What would it be like to be unable to use your arms or your legs? To be in a wheelchair? To be blind? To be unable to hear or speak?" "What would you need in order to be able to live a full and independent life?" Brainstorm and list what the special needs of people with disabilities are. Then read the introductory paragraph on page 88.

Suggested activities

- Read the sections about 'Meeting the needs of people with disabilities' on page 88. Hold a class discussion and encourage students to talk about people they know who have disabilities and how their needs are met.

- Encourage groups to discuss the questions in 'Transport and access in your area' (page 88), to keep notes of their discussions and to report their suggestions in a class discussion. Then ask them to work together to draft a letter to the local paper, explaining any problems they have identified and making suggestions about what could be done about them.

- Read the two newspaper articles on page 89. Ask students to talk about people they know with disabilities who have achieved successes, and about famous people with disabilities and their achievements (e.g. Home Secretary David Blunkett, physicist and author Stephen Hawking, and wheelchair athlete Tanni Grey-Thompson). Discuss how much media coverage is given to people with disabilities. Is it true that they are 'largely invisible' because they are under-represented on TV, newspapers and magazines?

Plenary

Conclude by discussing these two myths: 1) People with disabilities can't take care of themselves; 2) People with disabilities can't have successful careers. Discuss how with the right support and facilities, people with disabilities are quite capable of leading full, independent lives and achieving success.

Extension activities

Ask the students to invite someone with a disability to come and talk to the class. Prepare for the visit by getting them to draw up a list of questions they want to ask.

Suggest students interview a person with a disability, and to write an article about them based on the interview. Collect the articles into a booklet.

Recording and evaluating

Ask students to fill in the appropriate section of Copymaster R3 to record and evaluate what they have learned from this unit.

Your Life 1/Year 7

UNIT 19 You and global issues – resources, waste and recycling

Your Life 1/Year 7

Lesson 1 *Your Life 1*, pages 90–91
National Curriculum Programme of Study for Citizenship coverage 1i, 2a, 2b, 2c; links with QCA exemplar units 1, 10

Objective: To understand why reducing waste is a global issue and to discuss the benefits of recycling.

Resources

Copies of Copymaster 19 'Are you a waste watcher?' (*Your Life 1 Copymasters*, page 31)

Copies of Copymaster 8A 'Understanding recycling' (page 164)

Starter

Explain that we live in a throwaway society. Each year, every household throws away on average one tonne of rubbish. Ask: "What happens to our rubbish?" Explain that most of it is either dumped as landfill or burned in incinerators. Discuss what recycling is and how much of our rubbish consists of paper, metal and plastics that could be recycled.

Suggested activities

- Read 'Stop talking rubbish, start thinking about reducing waste' and 'Recycling facts' (page 90). Challenge pairs to show understanding of the articles by making a list of ten key facts they learn from the articles about waste and recycling.

- Read 'Reduce, re-use and recycle' (page 91). Discuss the five reasons with the class, then ask groups to do activity 2 (see 'In groups', page 91). Ask a reporter from each group to explain their plans to the rest of the class.

- Invite groups to do activity 1 (see 'In groups', page 91), to list their ideas and then to discuss as a class what they could do at home to reduce the amount of waste they throw away.

Plenary

Ask individuals to make a short statement answering 'Why I am concerned about waste' and to list their reasons on the board.

Extension activities

Ask students to design a poster to encourage young people to get involved in recycling.

Challenge individuals to complete the quiz on Copymaster 19, to check their scores, then to discuss in pairs what each of them needs to do to become more of a 'waste watcher'.

Ask students to use the internet to find out further information on recycling. Visit the websites of pressure groups, such as Friends of the Earth (www.foe.co.uk).

Assessment

Use Copymaster 8A to assess understanding of recycling.

Answers: Across – 1. green, 2. reduce, 4. pollution, 5. skip, 6. energy, 9. cans, 11. plastic 13. incinerator. Down – 1. gases, 3. conserve, 4. paper, 7. glass, 8. recycle, 10. acid, 12. iron.

UNIT 19 You and global issues – resources, waste and recycling

Your Life 1/Year 7

Lesson 2 *Your Life 1*, pages 92–93
National Curriculum Programme of Study for Citizenship coverage 1i, 2a, 2b, 2c, 3b

Objective: To carry out an audit of how the school manages its waste and to discuss setting up a school recycling scheme.

Resources

Copies of Copymaster R4 'Developing as a citizen' (page 184)

Starter

Explain that the first step towards developing a school recycling scheme is to carry out an audit. Read and discuss 'Becoming waste watchers – a waste audit' (page 92).

Suggested activities

● Challenge groups to design a questionnaire to carry out a waste audit, and then to work together to agree a class questionnaire.

● Read 'Working against waste' (page 92). Ask groups to discuss the four schemes and to suggest which of the four (if any) they think would be a suitable scheme for the school to develop. Then ask them to share their views in a class discussion.

● Read 'Setting up a school recycling scheme' (page 93). As a class talk about which materials are most suitable for collecting and why. Discuss what they need to find out in order to arrange their collection by a waste collector, and what they need to consider when deciding how to collect and store the materials on the school premises. Then ask groups to draft a plan for a school recycling scheme.

Plenary

Share some of their plans and discuss whether or not their plan is workable.

Extension activities

Develop a class proposal for a recycling scheme. Appoint a Waste Watchers committee. Ask the committee to conduct the audit by carrying out the questionnaire, analysing the findings and reporting them in a class discussion.

Redraft the groups' plans for a recycling scheme for the school, taking into consideration the findings of the audit. Discuss them as a class and decide on a class proposal to put to the rest of the school.

Ask students to draft a letter addressed to everyone in the school community, explaining why they think the school should introduce a recycling scheme and explaining their class proposal.

Recording and evaluating

Invite students to use the appropriate section of Copymaster R4 to record and evaluate what they have learned from this unit.

Your Life 1/Year 7

UNIT 20 You and your achievements – reviewing your progress

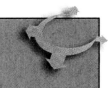

Your Life 1/Year 7

Lesson 1 *Your Life 1*, pages 94–95
National Framework for PSHE coverage 1a; National Curriculum Programme of Study for Citizenship coverage 3c; links with QCA exemplar unit 19

Objective: To review your progress and achievements in Year 7 and to set yourself targets for the future.

Resources

Copies of Copymaster 20 'Key skills' (*Your Life 1 Copymasters*, page 32)

Copies of Copymaster R1 'Understanding yourself' (page 181)

Starter

Explain that the lesson is the first part of a three-step process: 1) Thinking about your achievements; 2) Discussing your achievements and progress with your tutor and setting targets for Year 8; 3) Writing a statement for your Progress File.

Suggested activities

- Read 'Your subjects' (page 94) and ask the students to use the five-star system to give themselves grades, before writing a statement about their progress in each subject.

- Read 'Your key skills' (page 94) and ask the students to study Copymaster, then to write a statement reviewing their progress in each of the key skills.

- Read 'Your activities' (page 94) and ask the students to write a statement about their most significant achievements in their activities during the year.

- Read 'Your attitude and behaviour' (page 95) and ask the students to write a statement summing up their attitude and behaviour during the year.

Plenary

Allocate times for individuals to meet with you to discuss their statements and set targets, allowing them further time in tutor time (as necessary) to complete their statements.

Extension activities

Hold the discussion meetings with individuals. During the discussion, encourage them to note down any points you make, especially when agreeing targets at the end of the discussion (see 'Discussing your progress'/'Setting targets', page 95).

Ask the students to draft statements to go in their Record of Achievements (see 'Recording your achievements', page 95).

Recording and evaluating

Ask students to fill in the appropriate section of Copymaster R1 to record and evaluate what they have learned from this unit.

UNIT 1 You and your feelings – self-esteem

Your Life 2/Year 8

Lesson 1 *Your Life 2*, pages 6–7
National Framework for PSHE coverage 1a, 1c, 3c

Objective: To understand what self-esteem is, why it is important and how to build up self-esteem.

Starter

Write these words on the board: 'self-esteem', 'self-confidence', 'self-centredness', 'self-consciousness', 'self-importance' and 'self-possession'. Explain to the students what they mean, then draw two columns and list those which describe positive qualities (self-esteem, self-confidence and self-possession) and those which describe negative qualities (self-centredness, self-consciousness and self-importance). Then read 'Self-esteem" (page 6). Discuss why self-esteem is important and how having self-esteem is different from being conceited.

Suggested activities

- Explain that identifying your strong points is one way you can build up your self-esteem. Ask individuals to make lists of their own strengths and weaknesses, then to discuss them in pairs (see 'Know yourself' page 6).

- Read 'Feeling confident' (page 6) and Erica Stewart's tips on how to build your self-esteem (page 7). Invite groups to discuss Erica Stewart's advice and to report their ideas in a class discussion. Then, with the class, read and discuss 'David's story' (page 7).

- Ask groups to discuss the six statements in 'What do you think?' (page 7), to say why they agree or disagree with the statements, then to share their views in a class discussion.

Plenary

Recap the importance of developing self-esteem by asking students to suggest the reasons why self-esteem is important and listing them on the board. Talk about how people with high self-esteem are likely to be happier and to get into less trouble than those with low self-esteem. Explain how having low self-esteem can lead people into trouble by acting foolishly in order to try to impress other people and win popularity, or by taking out their negative feelings about themselves through bullying or other forms of antisocial behaviour.

Extension activity

Ask individuals to write statements aimed at building up their self-image by reflecting on positive aspects of themselves:

Eight Positive Things About Myself

Two things people say they like about me

Two things which I'm good at

Two things I've successfully achieved

Two reasons friends value my friendship

Individuals can then choose whether to share what they write with others or to keep it confidential.

Your Life 2/Year 8

UNIT 1 You and your feelings – self-esteem

Your Life 2/Year 8

Lesson 2 *Your Life 2*, pages 8–9
National Framework for PSHE coverage 1a, 1c, 3c

Objective: To develop self-confidence by discussing what causes shyness and how to cope with it and how to deal with and learn from mistakes.

Resources:

Copies of Copymaster 1 'Say goodbye to being shy!' (*Your Life 2 Copymasters*, page 13)

Copies of Copymaster R5 'Understanding yourself' (page 185)

Starter

Write the words 'introvert' and 'extrovert' on the board and explain that an introvert is someone who is inward looking, quiet, thoughtful and often rather shy, while an extrovert is outward looking, lively, boisterous and outgoing. Talk about how no one is a complete introvert or extrovert. Explain that if you're more of an extrovert you probably find coping with social situations easier than if you're more of an introvert. However, whatever type of person you are, there are times when you may feel shy or embarrassed, so you need to know how to deal with such feelings.

Suggested activities

- Read 'Coping with shyness' (page 8). Ask groups to discuss situations in which people are likely to feel shy and the advice on how to deal with shyness, then to share their ideas in a class discussion.

- Read the articles on 'Coping with classroom mistakes' and 'Learning from your mistakes' (page 9). Ask groups to identify three key pieces of advice given in the articles and to explain in a class discussion why they think those are the most important points.

- Read the statement about 'Apologising' (page 9) and discuss as a class whether they agree or disagree with it.

Plenary

Ask individuals to write a short statement for their files about making mistakes, explaining what they have learned about how to cope with mistakes. Then invite some of them to share their statements with the rest of the class.

Extension activity

Read the article 'Say goodbye to being shy!' on Copymaster 1. Ask groups to discuss the advice, then to demonstrate what they have learned about how to cope with shyness by preparing replies to the two letters, offering advice on how to overcome shyness.

Recording and evaluating

Ask students to fill in the appropriate section of Copymaster R5 to record and evaluate what they learned from this unit.

UNIT 2 You and your body – drugs and drugtaking

Your Life 2/Year 8

Lesson 1 *Your Life 2*, pages 10–11
National Framework for PSHE coverage 2d

Objective: To explore myths about drugtaking, and to understand the risks of taking cannabis and taking ecstasy.

Starter

Explain what a myth is (something which people believe which is not fact but fiction) and that there are lots of myths about drugs and drugtaking. Tell the students that you are going to read an article about drug myths. Before giving out the books, read out the four statements from 'Drugs – facts and fictions' (page 10). Ask each student to write down whether or not they think each statement is a myth or not.

Suggested activities

- Look at 'Drugs – facts and fictions' (page 10) and check whether or not students answered correctly. Then read the article, pausing after each section to discuss the comments on the statement. Emphasise that anyone who takes drugs is gambling with their health.

- Read 'Is cannabis safe?' (page 10). Then ask pairs, working with the books closed, to write down three effects that heavy use of cannabis can have.

- Ask pairs to read and study 'Ecstasy factfile' (page 11) and to make a list of the most important facts explained in the article. Then discuss as a class what the risks of taking ecstasy are.

Plenary

Hold a class discussion in which you discuss the statements of the three young people (see 'In groups', page 11).

Extension activities

Ask pairs to role play either the scene between two teenagers or the scene between the doctor and a teenager (see 'Role play', page 11).

Challenge individuals to demonstrate their knowledge and understanding of ecstasy by writing an article for a teenage magazine, entitled 'Ecstasy – is it worth the risk?' In addition to using the information on these pages, ask them to find out more about ecstasy by researching it on the internet, using websites such as www.drugscope.org.uk.

Organise a visit from a police officer to discuss drugs and drugtaking with the class. Before the visit, ask students to prepare questions to ask and, afterwards, hold a discussion about what they learned from the visit.

Your Life 2/Year 8

UNIT 2 You and your body – drugs and drugtaking

Lesson 2 *Your Life 2*, pages 12–13
National Framework for PSHE coverage 2d, 2g

Objective: To understand the laws about drugs and to explore how to deal with pressure to experiment with drugs.

Resources

Copies of Copymaster 2 'Should cannabis be legalised?' (*Your Life 2 Copymasters*, page 14)

Copies of Copymaster R6 'Keeping healthy' (page 186)

Starter

Introduce the topic by discussing the difference between drugs that are legal and drugs that are illegal. Remind students of the distinction between medicinal drugs (drugs prescribed by doctors and drugs considered safe enough to be sold as medicines at chemist's, e.g. aspirin), social drugs (drugs in everyday use which are not illegal – caffeine, nicotine, alcohol) and illegal drugs (drugs which it is against the law to possess because they are considered dangerous).

Suggested activities

● Read 'Drugs and the law' (page 12). Ask individuals to write answers to questions 1–4 (see 'In groups', page 12). Then ask them to discuss questions 5 and 6 in groups and to report their views in a class discussion, before writing their answers to those two questions.

● Introduce the issue of peer pressure to experiment with drugs by asking the students to imagine a teenager, Zed, who is at a party. Ask: "How might his friends put pressure on him to try drugs? What might they say or do?" "What can Zed say or do to resist this pressure?" Then read and discuss 'How to turn down drugs and stay friends' (page 13). Ask students to work individually to write down the piece of advice they think is the most helpful, then to share their views in a group or class discussion.

● Ask groups to show their understanding of how to say no to drugs by acting out or scripting a scene in which a teenager, like Zed, resists the pressure from a group of friends to experiment with a drug.

Plenary

Ask groups to act or read out their scenes and discuss which of the tactics used to say no they think are the most effective.

Extension activity

Read Copymaster 2. Explain the recent downgrading of cannabis from a Class B to a Class C drug. Then organise a debate on the issue of the law concerning cannabis.

Recording and evaluating

Ask students to fill in the appropriate section of Copymaster R6 to record and evaluate what they have learned from this unit.

UNIT 3 You and your responsibilities – other cultures and other lifestyles

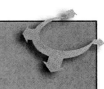

Your Life 2/Year 8

Lesson 1 *Your Life 2*, pages 14–15
National Framework for PSHE coverage 3a; National Curriculum Programme of Study for Citizenship coverage 1b; links with QCA exemplar unit 4

Objective: To understand that the United Kingdom is a diverse society, and to explore what ethnic stereotyping is and how it creates a false image of people.

Starter

Explain what 'multicultural' means and how in Britain today there are people from many cultures with different ideas, beliefs, values and traditions. Talk about how these people come from different ethnic groups, explaining that an ethnic group has racial, religious, linguistic and other features in common, and that Britain is a diverse society, in which there are people from many different ethnic groups. Explain how people have been coming to Britain for centuries and that the make up of present-day society is a result of the immigration that took place during the 20th century.

Suggested activities

- Read 'Britain – a diverse society' (page 14). Ask individuals to make notes on what it tells them about a) immigration after the Second World War and b) the ethnic population of Great Britain. Then, as a class, discuss what they have learned from the article.

- Ask students: "What are the benefits of living in a diverse society?" Ask them individually to think about such things as food, clothes, music, art, festivals, sport, travel and people, and to write one or two sentences saying what they like best about living in a diverse society. Then share their views in a class discussion.

- Explain what ethnic stereotyping is (thinking that a person behaves in a particular way because they belong to a certain ethnic group). Read the paragraph 'Ethnic stereotyping', the comments by Nazrah and Tariq and the poem 'Stereotype' (page 15). Ask groups to do the three discussion activities (see 'In groups', page 15), then to share their views in a class discussion.

Plenary

Recap what ethnic stereotyping is and discuss the negative effects it can have by sticking inappropriate labels on people.

Extension activity

Ask students to think of people from ethnic minorities who have made significant contributions to society. Build up a list on the board, e.g. broadcasters Trevor McDonald and Moira Stewart, actress Meera Syal, novelist Narinder Dhami, sports stars Denise Lewis, Jason Robinson and Rio Ferdinand, and rap poet Benjamin Zephaniah. Ask students to choose a person from an ethnic minority who has achieved success and to research what they have achieved on the internet, and then to explain to the rest of the class why they admire them. The 100 Black Britons campaign could be one starting point (www.100greatblackbritons.com).

Your Life KS3 Co-ordinator's File © *HarperCollinsPublishers* Ltd 2005. This page may be photocopied for use in the classroom.

Your Life 2/Year 8

Your Life 2/Year 8

Lesson 2 *Your Life 2*, pages 16–17
National Framework for PSHE coverage 3a; National Curriculum Programme of Study for Citizenship coverage 1b, 1h, 2a, 3a; links with QCA exemplar units 4, 9

Objective: To investigate images and stereotypes of ethnic groups in the media.

Resources

Copies of Copymaster 3 'Images of the Third World' (*Your Life 2 Copymasters*, page 15)

Copies of Copymaster R7 'Developing relationships' (page 187)

Starter

Remind them what stereotyping is (see Lesson 1). Explain what negative stereotyping is and note that it may occur as a result of how people are presented in the media. Ask: "Can you think of any examples of people from an ethnic minority being stereotyped in the TV programmes you watch?" Explain that the focus of the lesson is on the images of ethnic minorities presented in the media.

Suggested activities

● Read 'Films and TV programmes' (page 16). Ask: "What does the article tell you about negative stereotyping in films in the past?" Talk about how the stereotyping has changed. Ask: "Is it true that films now present a range of characters from ethnic minorities, rather than just stereotypes?" Talk about film stars from ethnic minorities and the roles they have played in recent films.

● Read 'TV "failing to reflect multicultural society"' (page 16). Discuss as a class the points it makes and invite them to give examples from their own TV viewing to explain why they agree or disagree with what the article says. Ask groups to carry out activity 4 (see 'In groups', page 16) and to write out their plans, then to explain them to the rest of the class.

● Read 'A distorted picture' (page 17) and 'The Press' (page 17). Discuss as a class what the articles say about the media's image of India and Indians. Ask: "What image does the media give of Africa and Africans?" "What do you think TV companies and newspapers should be doing to make sure they do not reinforce stereotyping?" Challenge students to show their understanding of the issues raised on this page by writing a letter expressing their views. **AO**

Plenary

Study 'Only joking?' (page 17) and discuss how racial jokes reinforce stereotyping.

Extension activities

Read the statements on Copymaster 3. Ask groups to discuss the questions, then to share their ideas in a class discussion.

Recording and evaluating

Ask the students to fill in the appropriate section of Copymaster R7 to record and evaluate what they have learned from this unit.

UNIT 4 You and your money – gambling

Your Life 2/Year 8

Lesson 1 *Your Life 2*, pages 18–19
National Framework for PSHE coverage 1g

Objective: To examine the reasons why people gamble, to explain the laws about gambling and to explore attitudes towards gambling.

Starter

Introduce the topic by asking the students: "Why do people gamble?" Ask pairs to write down all the reasons they can think of, then encourage them to share their ideas in a class discussion and list their ideas on the board.

Suggested activities

- Read 'Gambling – the lure and the law' (page 18). Compare the list of reasons why young people gamble with the list you made on the board. Then discuss the law on gambling. Ask: "Is it too easy for young people to gamble?" "Should there be tighter restrictions or should there be no restrictions on young people gambling?"

- Focus on fruit machines. Ask: "What's the attraction of fruit machines?" "Why do some young people spend a lot of money on them?" Read 'Fruit machine facts' (page 19), before asking the students to design a poster, based on the information in the article, with a slogan such as 'Don't be mugged by fruit machines'.

- Read 'Winners and losers" and "The National Lottery (page 19). Then ask groups to discuss their views about the National Lottery before sharing them in a class discussion.

Plenary

Talk about how gambling is regarded as a sin in some religions. Ask: "What are the moral and religious arguments against gambling?" Make a list on the board, e.g.:

Gambling is a sin because you should trust in God, not chance, to provide your needs.

Gambling is wrong because you win money by luck rather than earning it.

Gambling causes misery because it can lead people into debt.

People spend money on gambling which could be better spent in other ways.

Gambling can be addictive and lead people to steal to fund their habit.

Gambling can make people cheat and lie.

Discuss each argument in turn and get students to say why they agree or disagree with it.

Extension activities

Organise a class debate: 'This class believes that all forms of gambling should be banned'.

Ask individuals to write a statement expressing their views on gambling (see 'For your file', page 18).

UNIT 4 You and your money – gambling

Your Life 2/Year 8

Lesson 2 *Your Life 2*, pages 20–21
National Framework for PSHE coverage 1g

> **Objective:** To investigate problem gambling and to discuss responsible gambling.

Resources

Copies of Copymaster 4 'Gambling problems' (*Your Life 2 Copymasters,* page 16)

Copies of Copymaster R5 'Understanding yourself' (page 185)

Starter

Explain what the terms 'obsession' and 'addiction' mean, and how some people become obsessed with and addicted to gambling. Tell the students that the focus of the lesson is on gambling problems. Talk about how problem-gamblers spend their time and money (which could be spent on other things) on gambling. Introduce the concept of opportunity cost and tell them to think about what the opportunity cost of their gambling is to the two young people whose stories they are going to read.

Suggested activities

- Read 'Gambling has taken over my life' (page 20) and discuss in groups, then as a class, the effects that gambling had on Keri's life and on Jason's life. Ask: "What else did Keri and Jason lose, besides money, as a result of their gambling?" Talk about how it led to a loss of self-respect because they started stealing, and how it affected their relationships with friends and family. Then suggest individuals write a similar story about a teenage gambler and the problems gambling caused in their lives, entitled 'I wish I'd never started gambling'.

- Read 'Problem gambling' (page 21). Talk about how you can tell if someone has a gambling problem and what you can do if you think a friend has a problem. Then read 'Responsible gambling' (page 21) and discuss the advice on how to gamble responsibly.

Plenary

Conclude the lesson with a review of the students' attitudes towards gambling by encouraging them to explain in a class discussion why they agree or disagree with the two statements about gambling (see 'In groups', page 21).

Extension activities

Invite the students to show their understanding of gambling problems by reading and discussing the letters on Copymaster 4, then drafting replies.

Act out the role plays (see Role play, page 21), suggesting students practise saying "No" by taking it in turns to be the odd one out.

Recording and evaluating

Ask the students to fill in the appropriate section of Copymaster R5 to record and evaluate what they have learned from this unit.

UNIT 5 You and your values – where do you stand?

Your Life 2/Year 8

Lesson 1 *Your Life 2*, pages 22–23
National Curriculum Programme of Study for Citizenship coverage 2a, 2b, 2c

Objective: To understand how your beliefs and values influence the way you behave, what your ambitions are and who you admire.

Resources

Copies of Copymaster 5 'What influences how you behave?' (*Your Life 2 Copymasters*, page 17)

Starter

Talk about how your behaviour is influenced by what your beliefs and values are. Ask the students: "What's the most important thing that influences you when making a decision about how to behave?" "Is it: a) What your parents will think? b) Whether or not you'll get into trouble? c) Whether or not it's right or wrong? d) Whether or not you'll benefit from your actions? e) Whether or not your actions will hurt someone?" Ask each of them to write a short statement saying what most influences how they behave.

Suggested activities

- Ask individuals to do the ranking activity 'What influences how you behave?' (see page 22 or use Copymaster 5). Then ask them to share their views in a group discussion, comparing their statements with what other group members think should be the most important influences.

- Study the list of things which young people said were important when asked to state their ambitions (see 'Your ambitions', page 22). Ask students to discuss the list and to share their views on what they consider to be important.

- Read the article 'Idols or heroes?' (page 23). Ask groups to discuss whether or not they agree with Derek Stuart's views, to decide on their definition of a hero and to propose some heroes to include in a class 'Hall of fame'. Then hold a class discussion and agree a class list of top ten heroes.

- Ask individuals to think about someone they know personally whom they admire (see 'Someone I admire', page 23) and to explain to a partner who it is and why they admire the person.

Plenary

Talk about how society often rewards pop stars, TV personalities and sports stars more than people who make other contributions to society, such as nurses, doctors, police officers and fire officers. Ask: "Has society got its values right? Who should we value more – the Premier League footballer or the ambulance driver?"

Extension activity

Suggest individuals write a letter to the editor of the magazine in which 'Idols or heroes?' (page 23) might have appeared, replying to Derek Stuart's views and saying why they agree or disagree with them.

Your Life 2/Year 8

UNIT 5 You and your values – where do you stand?

Lesson 2 *Your Life 2*, pages 24–25
National Curriculum Programme of Study for Citizenship coverage 2a, 2b, 2c

---

Objective: To consider some of the issues that make news and to discuss which are the most important.

Resources

Copies of Copymaster 9A 'Understanding your values' (page 165)

Copies of Copymaster R8 'Developing as a citizen' (page 188)

Starter

Ask the students: "What are the major issues that face us in the world today?" Make a list of their suggestions on the board, e.g. terrorism, global warming, poverty, cloning, deforestation, pollution, AIDS, human rights, weapons of mass destruction and racism. Ask: "If you had £10 million to spend on one of these issues, which would you choose to spend it on?" Invite them to share their views in a class discussion. Talk about how their views differ according to their values and beliefs.

Suggested activities

- Explain that the class is going to do a ranking exercise. Ask pairs to read and study the reports on pages 24–25, then to rank them in order of the importance of the issue they raise. Ask them to compare their views in a class discussion, inviting individuals to explain why they consider some issues to be more important than others.

- Ask individuals to choose one of the issues on which they have a strong opinion and to write a letter expressing their views on the issue.

Plenary

Share some of their letters.

Extension activities

Choose an issue that particularly interests the class. Suggest they research the issue on the internet and then either to organise a debate on the issue or to role play a TV discussion of the issue.

Ask students to cut out newspaper reports that raise issues about which they are concerned and to write comments expressing their opinions on the issues. Ask the students either to put them in their files or to mount them and make a display on topical issues.

Assessment

Use Copymaster 9A to assess understanding of what their values are.

Recording and evaluating

Ask the students to use the appropriate section of Copymaster R8 to help them to record and evaluate what they have learned from this unit.

UNIT 6 You and your family – divided families

> **Objective:** To explore the reasons why parents separate and the feelings that this can cause and to understand who decides whom children live with.

Resources

Copies of Copymaster 6 'It's all my fault!' (*Your Life 2 Copymasters*, page 18)

Starter

Introduce the topic by setting ground rules for discussion and stressing that no one needs to talk about their own experiences if they do not want to. Explain that there are many reasons why relationships break up. What different reasons can the class think of? Make a list on the board, such as: money problems, affairs, domestic violence, drug or alcohol addiction, incompatibility or stress (caused by unemployment, bereavement, long-term illness or unfulfilled expectations). Discuss how there are often a combination of factors, rather than one single cause.

Suggested activities

- Read 'Dealing with divorce' (page 26). Ask groups to discuss what the three children say about their parents' divorce and then share their views in a class discussion.

- Ask individuals to study the eight statements in 'What do you think?' (page 26), to write down whether or not they agree with them, then to share their views in a group discussion.

- Read 'A mixture of feelings' (page 27). Discuss with the class the different feelings that the young people describe. Ask: "Who is the best person to talk to about your feelings?"

- Read 'Who decides who you live with?' (page 27). Make sure students understand what a residence order and a contact order are. Invite pairs to discuss the view that children should always have the final say. Ask: "Does it depend how old the child is?" Then hold a class discussion in which the students share their views.

Plenary

Discuss Pat's letter (see 'For your file', page 27) with the class and list the main points that they would include in their reply. End by re-emphasising that there are many reasons why parents split up, but that children are not to blame if they do.

Extension activity

Ask pairs and then groups to discuss the comments on Copymaster 6. As a class, discuss what you can say and do to help a friend who is experiencing such thoughts and feelings.

UNIT 6 You and your family – divided families

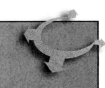

Your Life 2/Year 8

Lesson 2 *Your Life 2*, pages 28–29
National Framework for PSHE coverage 1d, 3e, 3f, 3g

Objective: To explore the changes that occur when parents separate and to examine living in a stepfamily.

Resources

Copies of Copymaster R7 'Developing relationships' (page 187)

Starter

Explain the focus of the lesson. Talk about the changes that can occur when parents separate, e.g. having to move house or school, living with only one parent or in a stepfamily, having less money or having to take on more household chores, having to make contact arrangements to see the parent you don't live with or losing contact with them. Then read the introductory paragraph on page 28.

Suggested activities

- Read and discuss in groups the experiences of Barbara, Chris and Xanthe (page 28). Then ask groups to discuss the issues regarding keeping contact with the absent parent and whether or not to tell friends what is happening. Share their views in a class discussion.

- Ask the students: "What problems do children face when settling into a stepfamily?" Read and discuss with the class the three statements in the section 'Living in a stepfamily' (page 29). Talk about any other problems and difficulties that members of the class suggest stepchildren may face.

- Ask individuals to study the article 'How to cope with step-parents' (page 29) and to make their own notes on the advice it gives on how to deal with step-parents and on how to get on with step-siblings. Then ask groups to draw up a list of their top tips on how to survive in a stepfamily and to share their lists in a class discussion.

Plenary

Summarise what the students have learned from these two lessons about how to deal with separation, divorce and living in a stepfamily by drawing up a list of 'Dos' and 'Don'ts' on how to cope when parents split up.

Extension activities

Ask students to show their understanding of the feelings a person can experience when joining a step-family by writing a reply to Jan's letter (see 'For your file', page 29).

Encourage students to read and write reviews of books which offer information and advice on the topic, such as *Caught in the Middle* by Alys Swan-Jackson (Piccadilly) and novels which deal with the issues, such as Anne Fine's *Step by Wicked Step* (Puffin).

Recording and evaluating

Ask students to fill in the appropriate section of Copymaster R7 to record and evaluate what they learned from this unit.

UNIT 7 You and your safety – at home and in the street

Your Life 2/Year 8

Lesson 1 *Your Life 2*, pages 30–31
National Framework for PSHE coverage 2h

Objective: To understand how to give basic first aid for cuts, fractures, burns and scalds.

Starter

Explain that more people are injured in accidents at home than anywhere else. Ask the students to share experiences of accidents at home involving them, their family or friends. Discuss what happened and the causes, and whether there was anybody on hand who could give first aid. Explain that the commonest types of accidents are falls, and that among the most serious are those that cause severe bleeding. Point out how important it is to know how to give first aid.

Suggested activities

- Ask pairs to read and study 'First aid for cuts', 'What to do if someone falls' and 'First aid for fractures' on page 30. Then ask them to write answers to the four questions (see 'In pairs', page 30).

- Read 'First aid for burns and scalds' (page 31). Then challenge pairs to test each other's understanding by closing the book and taking it in turns to explain the six things to do when dealing with a burn or scald.

- Read 'What to do if the house is on fire' (page 31) and, in a class discussion, make sure the students understand the reasons for each of the actions you should take. Then talk about potential fire hazards in the home and read and discuss the information in 'Chip pans' (page 31).

Plenary

Test the students' understanding of first-aid procedures by giving them a ten-question quiz based on the information on pages 30–31.

AO

Extension activities

Ask students to design a poster offering safety advice (see 'For your file', page 31).

Suggest students use the resources centre and the internet to find out about first aid for other accidental injuries (e.g. suffocating or choking), and to write out sets of instructions explaining what you should do to treat them.

Ask groups to draw up plans for a short information video on first aid in the home. Then allow them to present their proposals to the rest of the class.

Invite a member of the local St John Ambulance to come and give a demonstration of first-aid procedures.

Your Life 2/Year 8

UNIT 7 You and your safety – at home and in the street

Your Life 2/Year 8

Lesson 2 *Your Life 2*, pages 32–33
National Framework for PSHE coverage 2g

> **Objective:** To understand what child abuse is and what victims of child abuse should do.

Starter

Introduce the topic by defining what child abuse is: when adults hurt children either physically or in some other way. Explain that sexual abuse is only one form of child abuse. Ask: "What other forms of child abuse can you think of?" List types of abuse on the board, e.g. physical punishment of children i.e. hitting or spanking; neglecting children by not feeding them/changing their clothes; denying children their right to an education; forcing children to work, for example in factories; emotionally abusing children by constantly threatening them or putting them down; giving children drugs. Explain that child abuse occurs in all parts of the world, in both developed and less developed countries.

Suggested activities

- Read and discuss 'What is child abuse?' (page 32). Focus first on the kinds of abuse. Reinforce what has already been said about different types of abuse. Draw attention to the cartoon's point that parents are not abusing their children's rights by not letting them have their own way all the time, or in stopping them from doing something that may be unwise or unsafe. When discussing the paragraph 'Why does it happen?', emphasise the points made in the final sentence (abuse is always wrong and never the young person's fault).

- Explain that people have a range of views about smacking. Invite groups to discuss their views on smacking and on the statement that "a good hiding never did anybody any harm". Then share their views in a class discussion.

- Read 'Facts and fictions about abuse' (page 32) and the two articles about sexual abuse on page 33. Draw attention to key points: how the offender is often someone they know rather than a stranger; how victims feel guilty and ashamed but should try to concentrate on feeling angry and the importance of speaking out.

- After discussing the information in 'What happens next?' (page 33), stress that the consequences of not speaking out can be much more harmful than those of speaking out.

Plenary

Ask the class to suggest the most important things about child abuse that they learned from the lesson and make a list on the board.

Extension activity

Talk about the dangers of internet chat-rooms, of sending your picture via the internet to a stranger whose age you may not know and how abusers may try to use the internet to make contact with young people. Suggest groups draw up a set of guidelines on how to use the internet safely, in order to protect themselves from being abused.

UNIT 7 You and your safety – at home and in the street

Your Life 2/Year 8

Lesson 3 *Your Life 2*, pages 34–35
National Framework for PSHE coverage 2f; links with QCA citizenship

Objective: To explore how to stay safe when out and about in the street and in other public places.

Resources

Copies of Copymaster 7 'Be streetwise' (*Your Life 2 Copymasters,* page 19)

Starter

Introduce the topic by discussing how some places are safer than others (e.g. a well-lit street is safer than a dark underpass or a lonely country lane); how some times are safer than others (e.g. the rush-hour is safer than late at night); how some situations are safer than others (e.g. you're safer in a group than on your own and safer waiting for the last bus inside a café than on the pavement). Ask students to share their experiences of when they have felt unsafe and to consider what it was about the place, the time and the situation that made them feel unsafe. Explain that the aim of the lesson is to explore ways of staying safe when you are out and about.

Suggested activities

- Read 'Staying safe in the street' and 'Safety on buses' (page 34). In a class discussion talk about the reasons for each piece of advice. Can students suggest any other things to do/to avoid doing in order to stay safe in the street and on the buses?

- Ask groups to discuss the ten situations in 'What should you do if…?' (page 34), to write down what they decide you should do and then to share their views in a class discussion.

- Invite pairs to read and study 'Safety in public places' (page 35) and to summarise the advice given by making a list of 'Dos' and 'Don'ts'. Then discuss the advice in a class discussion.

Plenary

Ask individuals to write down what they think are the five most important things to do/to avoid doing in order to stay safe when they are out and about. Invite some of them to read their lists to the rest of the class.

Extension activities

Ask groups either to design a leaflet or produce plans for a video advising young people on how to stay safe in the street.

Ask pairs to draw up a 'Paper-round safety code', giving advice to young people with paper rounds. Then give out copies of Copymaster 7 and ask them to compare their advice with that given in the leaflet, produced by the Metropolitan Police. Then, as a class, read and discuss the advice on looking for work.

Your Life 2/Year 8

UNIT 7 You and your safety – at home and in the street

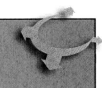

Your Life 2/Year 8

Lesson 4 *Your Life 2*, pages 36–37
National Framework for PSHE coverage 2h

> **Objective:** To provide information on road safety: to understand how to cycle safely, how to make an emergency telephone call and how to give emergency first aid.

Resources

Copies of Copymaster R6 'Keeping healthy' (page 186)

Starter

Explain that the most dangerous age for cyclists is 12 to 14. Talk about any accidents the students have been involved in as cyclists or seen involving cyclists. What happened? Is there anything the cyclist could have/should have done that would have prevented the accident or made it less serious? Ask the students to brainstorm the most vital piece of advice they would give young cyclists to help to protect them or to avoid accidents. List their ideas on the board.

Suggested activities

- Read 'Cycling safely' (page 36) with the class. Then ask the students to close their books and test them to see if they can remember the procedures to follow when turning right and at roundabouts, and what they should do when crossing the pavement and riding at night.

- Ask groups to discuss questions 1–3 (see 'In groups', page 36) and to share their ideas with rest of the class. Then give them the choice to do activities 4–6, in whichever order they would prefer.

- Go through the procedure for making an emergency telephone call (see page 36). Invite pairs to role play calling for an ambulance from a mobile (012 456 7890) for a teenage cyclist who has been knocked unconscious in an accident at the junction of High Street and Market Street in Oldtown town centre.

- Read 'Emergency first aid', 'Shock' and 'Unconsciousness' on page 37 and ask pairs to show their understanding of the information by explaining what to do with a person who is unconscious and how to treat shock. Then choose one of the pairs to demonstrate how to put someone into the recovery position.

Plenary

Explain that the priorities when giving emergency first aid are 'ABC'. First, check that the Airway isn't blocked. Then, check that the casualty is still Breathing. Thirdly, check Circulation by checking for a pulse. Then recap on how to put someone in the recovery position.

Extension activity

Ask students to use the internet (www.thinksafety.gov.uk) to research a highway code for young road users.

Recording and evaluating

Ask students to fill in the appropriate section of Copymaster R6 to record and evaluate what they learned from this unit.

Your Life 2/Year 8

Lesson 1 *Your Life 2*, pages 38–39
National Curriculum Programme of Study for Citizenship coverage 1a, 2a, 2b, 2c; links with QCA exemplar units 2, 15

Objective: To understand what powers the police have to stop and search and to question people, and to explain the system of reprimands, warnings and prosecutions.

Resources

Copies of Copymaster 8 'What are your rights?' (*Your Life 2 Copymasters*, page 20)

Copies of Copymaster 10A 'Understanding your rights' (page 166)

Starter

Introduce the topic by asking: "Why do we have a police force?" "What would happen if we did not have a police force?" "What are the police's duties and responsibilities?" List on the board what the class think the police's duties are, then read the first paragraph on page 38.

Suggested activities

- Read the rest of 'Police duties and police powers' (page 38). Hold a class discussion in which you talk about police powers and people's rights with regard to being stopped and searched, and how to behave if you are either stopped or searched. Then debate the two views expressed in the statements (see 'In groups', page 38).

- Read 'Helping the police' (page 39). Ask: "What are your rights if the police ask you to go to a police station and if they want to question you?" Make a list of the students' rights on the board.

- Read 'Reprimands, warnings and prosecutions' (page 39), stopping after each section to explain the information and to answer any questions. Then invite groups to carry out the discussion activity (see 'In groups', page 39) and to report their views in a class discussion.

Plenary

Recap on the system for dealing with young people who break the law, making sure that students understand the circumstances in which reprimands and warnings are given and in which prosecutions will take place. Remind students how long records are kept on young offenders and discuss what the consequences of having a record may be, e.g. when looking for a job.

Extension activity

Ask groups to discuss the rights of the three young people in the situations described on Copymaster 8. The answers are explained in the notes on Unit 8 on page 7 of *Your Life 2 Copymasters*.

Assessment

Use Copymaster 10A to assess understanding of their rights and the rights of the police. The answers are: 1. True, 2. False, 3. False, 4. True, 5. True, 6. True, 7. False, 8. True, 9. True, 10. False, 11. True, 12. False, 13. False, 14. True, 15. True.

Your Life 2/Year 8

UNIT 8 You and the law – the police

Your Life 2/Year 8

Lesson 2 *Your Life 2*, pages 40–41
National Curriculum Programme of Study for Citizenship coverage 1a, 2a, 2b, 2c; links with QCA exemplar units 2, 15

Objective: To explore the role of the police in maintaining public order, and to discuss attitudes towards the police.

Resources

Copies of a police recruitment advertisement (optional)

Copies of Copymaster R8 'Developing as a citizen' (page 188)

Starter

Explain that one of the duties of the police is to maintain public order by controlling crowds at public events such as concerts, sports events and demonstrations. Talk about how in a free society people have the right to demonstrate but they must not break certain laws by behaving violently, obstructing the highway, trespassing or causing a nuisance. Explain that the lesson will focus on how the police control large crowds and on attitudes towards the police.

Suggested activities

- Ask students to share their experiences of being in large crowds. Ask: "What do you think of the way the police controlled the crowd?" Then read 'Keeping the peace' (page 40). Ask: "Do you think the police sometimes over-react and spark off trouble at demonstrations?" Discuss the senior police officer's statement on page 40, and ask: "Are media reports of demonstrations distorted?" "Does media presence 'egg a crowd on'?"

- Read the article about raves (page 40). Ask groups to imagine that they are part of a local authority licensing committee, and are considering an application to hold a rave in an empty storage warehouse. They should discuss the things they would need to take into consideration when deciding whether or not to grant permission. Share the groups' views in a class discussion.

- Ask: "What do you think of the police?" Invite individuals to write down whether they agree/disagree/are not sure about each of the 12 statements on page 41, then to share their views in a group or class discussion.

- Read 'Doing a good job?' (page 41) and discuss what it says about police regulation and the disciplinary code a police officer must follow. Ask: "What qualities and abilities do you think a police officer needs to have?"

Plenary

Ask each student to write a short statement saying what they think about the police and why.

Extension activity

Show students a copy of a police recruitment advertisement. Ask: "Would you consider becoming a police officer?" Ask groups to list the advantages and disadvantages of a career in the police force, then hold a class discussion.

Recording and evaluating

Ask students to use the appropriate section of Copymaster R8 to help them to record and evaluate what they learned from this unit.

Your Life 2/Year 8

UNIT 9 You and other people – friends and friendships

Your Life 2/Year 8

Lesson 1 *Your Life 2*, pages 42–43
National Framework for PSHE coverage 3b, 3c, 3j, 3k

> **Objective:** To explore the nature of friendship, what makes a good friend and how to make and keep friends.

Starter

Ask: "What qualities do you value in a friend?" Ask pairs to make a list, e.g. honesty, loyalty, patience, tolerance, understanding, forgiveness, sense of humour, liveliness, sensitivity and tact. Encourage them to share their views in a class discussion and make a class list on the board.

Suggested activities

- Ask pairs to discuss the ten statements 'What is a friend?' (page 42), then to share their opinions in a group discussion.

- Read and discuss in groups 'The secret of making friends' (page 42). Then invite them to make lists of 'Dos' and 'Don'ts', giving advice on how to behave in order to make and keep friends.

- Read and discuss the article 'Growing apart' (page 43). Discuss as a class the advice it gives. Ask: "What other advice would you offer to someone who feels they are drifting apart from a friend?"

Plenary

Study 'The rules of friendship' (page 43). Ask the students to discuss whether they agree/disagree with the rules. Invite each student to write down which three rules they consider to be the most important, then to share their views.

Extension activities

Ask individuals to show what they have learned about friendship by writing their views on friends and friendships (see 'For your file', page 42).

Ask groups to draft a reply to this letter to a magazine's agony aunt: "I have difficulty in making friends. What advice can you give me?" M.

UNIT 9 You and other people – friends and friendships

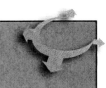

Your Life 2/Year 8

Lesson 2 *Your Life 2*, pages 44–45
National Framework for PSHE coverage 3b, 3c, 3i, 3j, 3k

Objective: To explore how friends may influence you, how groups behave and how to resist peer pressure.

Resources

Copies of Copymaster 9 'Staying in control of your life' (*Your Life 2 Copymasters,* page 21)

Copies of Copymaster R7 'Developing relationships' (page 187)

Starter

Ask the students: "How much do you think your friends influence you?" Suggest individuals use a five-point scale to rate how much influence they consider their friends have on the decisions they make (1 a lot, 2 quite a lot, 3 a fair amount, 4 not very much, 5 hardly any) and to write one or two sentences explaining the reasons for their view.

Suggested activities

- Ask individuals to complete the quiz on page 44. Then ask them to check what their answers tell them. Invite them to compare this with their rating of their friends' influence in a discussion with a partner.

- Hold a class discussion about gangs. Ask: "Why do people go round in gangs?" Discuss the way people talk and behave in gangs, and their experiences of gangs. Ask: "What's your opinion of gangs and how they behave?" Read 'Gangs – know the facts' (page 45) and discuss what the article says about gangs. Suggest individuals study the three statements about gangs on page 45, and then to write statements giving their own views.

- Ask pairs to act out the role plays in which one friend puts pressure on another friend to do something they do not want to do (see 'Role play', page 45). Then ask some of them to act out their role plays in front of the class and to discuss the strategies they use in order to resist pressure. **AO**

Plenary

Write the statements below on the board and encourage the students to discuss whether or not they agree with them:

> Friends who pressurise you all the time are not good friends.
> You have to let your friends influence you sometimes or you'll lose your friends.
> People who won't do what their friends want them to do are spoilsports.
> A real friend will respect your right to choose.

Extension activities

Read Copymaster 9. Discuss the advice it gives in groups, then ask them to share their views in a class discussion.

Ask groups to develop a role play or to script a scene about someone who allows a friend to pressurise them into doing something they later regret.

Recording and evaluating

Ask students to fill in the appropriate section of Copymaster R7 to record and evaluate what they learned from this unit.

UNIT 10 You and the media – the power of advertising

Your Life 2/Year 8

Lesson 1 *Your Life 2*, pages 46–47
National Curriculum Programme of Study for Citizenship coverage 1h, 2a, 2b; links with QCA exemplar unit 9

Objective: To discuss the power and influence of advertising and to understand the rules for advertisements which target children.

Resources

Copies of Copymaster 10 'Advertising issues' (*Your Life 2 Copymasters*, page 22)

Video recording of several TV commercials

Starter

Begin with a series of questions about brand names. Ask individuals to write down the name of the brand they associate with certain products, e.g. 1) crisps, 2) cola, 3) chocolate bars, 4) trainers, 5) mobile phones. Record their answers on the board and discuss which brand names occurred the most often and why. Discuss how much this is due to advertising and read the two introductory paragraphs about advertising on page 46.

Suggested activities

- Read 'Is advertising good or bad?' (page 46). Ask groups to draw up lists of the arguments in favour of advertising and against advertising. Then read 'In groups' (page 46) and invite them to share their views of the two statements in a class discussion.

- Read 'How much influence do adverts have on you?' (page 46). Then show the students the video of some recent TV commercials. In groups, ask them to talk about current TV advertisements. Which are the most popular? How effective are they? Do they just make you remember the product or do they actually influence you to buy it? In a class discussion, encourage the students to share their views on how much influence advertisements have.

- Read 'Advertising and children' (page 47). Ask pairs of students to study the Radio Authority guidelines and talk about the reasons for each rule. Then hold a class discussion of the Swedish view that all television adverts aimed at children should be banned throughout the EU.

Plenary

Recap the arguments for and against advertising. Ask the students to write a statement saying whether they agree with the view that advertising does more good than harm. Then invite some of them to read out their statements.

Extension activities

Read Copymaster 10 and ask groups to discuss their views on the portrayal of women and men in advertisements, and on the issue of whether people from ethnic minorities are under-represented in adverts. Then invite them to cut out advertisements from magazines showing women and men, to write comments on how they are portrayed in the adverts and to make a wall display of images and stereotypes in advertising.

Ask students to research how the advertising industry is regulated by using the internet (see www.asa.org.uk) to find out what the Advertising Standards Authority is and how it deals with complaints.

UNIT 10 You and the media – the power of advertising

Your Life 2/Year 8

Lesson 2 *Your Life 2*, pages 48–49
National Curriculum Programme of Study for Citizenship coverage 1h, 2a, 2b; links with QCA exemplar unit 9

Objective: To examine TV advertising, how TV and radio adverts are made and how advertisers use sponsorship and celebrity endorsements.

Resources

Video recording of several TV adverts

Copies of Copymaster 11A 'Understanding advertising' (page 167)

Copies of Copymaster R8 'Developing as a citizen' (page 188)

Starter

Show the class a TV advert for a product. Ask: "What image of the product is given?" Talk about how the image is created – by the setting, the type of people in it, the words used, and the music. Ask: "How much actual information about the product is given in the advert?" "How does the advert try to sell the product – by giving information and/or creating an image?"

Suggested activities

● Read 'The commercial break" (page 48). Ask groups to discuss what it says about TV adverts and to make a list of techniques used in TV adverts. Show them a further selection of TV adverts and discuss the techniques used in them.

● Read and discuss in groups what Bryony Gordon says in 'Celebrity endorsement' (page 49). Talk about current examples of celebrity endorsement. Are some more effective than others? Can they explain why?

● Read 'Sponsorship' (page 49). Debate the view that big companies should donate their money to charities and worthy causes, rather than spend huge sums on sponsorship. Discuss whether the publicity they would generate from doing so would be as effective as the publicity they get from sponsorship.

Plenary

Summarise how advertisers get their message across by asking: "What are the most effective adverts currently on TV?" "What techniques do they use a) to hold your attention and b) to get their message across?"

Extension activity

Ask students to find an advertisement in a newspaper or magazine and to show their understanding of advertising by writing an analysis of it (see 'For your file', page 48).

Assessment

Use Copymaster 11A to assess understanding of advertising.

Answers: Across – 1. stereotype, 5. jingle, 6. decent, 7. sport, 9. snack, 11. logo, 12. slogan, 13. legal, 16. ITC. Down – 1. Sweden, 2. revenue, 3. prices, 4. celebrity, 8. mail, 9. sponsor, 10. honest, 12. sales, 14. eat, 15. lead.

Recording and evaluating

Ask students to use the appropriate section of Copymaster R8 to help them to record and evaluate what they learned from this unit.

UNIT 11 You and your time – making the most of your leisure

Lesson 1 *Your Life 2*, pages 50–51
National Framework for PSHE coverage 1a, 2c; links with QCA citizenship exemplar unit 8

Objective: To explore the use they make of their leisure time.

Resources

Copies of Copymaster 11 'How do you use your leisure time?' (*Your Life 2 Copymasters*, page 23)

Starter

Ask the students: "How well do you think you use your leisure time?" "Are you good at planning how you use your leisure time? At getting involved in school and community activities? At using your leisure time constructively?" Ask individuals to rate their use of leisure time on a five-point scale (5 = excellent to 1 = poor) and to explain the reasons for their assessment.

Suggested activities

- Ask individuals to complete the quiz (see pages 50–51), then to check what their answers tell them about their use of leisure time, and to compare this with the assessment they made before doing the quiz. Ask them to discuss, in pairs, what they have learned from the activity, then ask each student to think of at least one way in which they can make better use of their leisure time.

- Read and discuss Peta's letter (page 51). In groups, share experiences of difficulties they have had as a result of not planning their use of leisure time and brainstorm ways of overcoming the problem. How can they improve their planning skills? Then draft a reply to Peta's letter.

Plenary

Read 'Four ways to make better use of your leisure time' (page 51). Ask: "What other things can you suggest people could do to make better use of their leisure time?" Make a list on the board of their suggestions. Then invite individuals to draw up an action plan for making better use of their leisure time a) during the week, b) at weekends.

Extension activity

Ask groups to prepare a questionnaire to survey how members of the class spend their weekends. Then give the questionnaire to another group to complete. Ask them to analyse their findings and report them to the rest of the class.

UNIT 11 You and your time – making the most of your leisure

Lesson 2 *Your Life 2*, pages 52–53
National Framework for PSHE coverage 1a, 2c; links with QCA citizenship exemplar unit 8

Objective: To explore ways of using leisure time constructively, and to discuss the importance of exercise and to compare the benefits of different types of exercise.

Resources

Copies of Copymaster R5 'Understanding yourself' (page 185)

Starter

Ask the students: "Why is exercise good for you?" List the reasons on the board: Physical benefits – it strengthens the heart and keeps the circulatory system working efficiently; it keeps the lungs and respiratory system working well; it keeps muscles in good condition; it stops you getting overweight. Mental benefits – it relaxes you and helps get rid of tension; it's good for self-esteem because it keeps your body in good shape.

Suggested activities

- Read 'Choose your exercise' (page 53). Discuss with the class what the S-factors are and why each is important. Then ask pairs to study the S-factor score chart, to work out a test-yourself quiz, and to give it to another pair to complete.

- Ask: "How would you convince someone that exercise is good for you and not a waste of time?" Suggest the students note down the arguments suggested and then to show their understanding of them by drafting a reply to Sam's letter (see 'For your file', page 53).

- Read about how to beat the boredom blues ('Getting a piece of the action', page 52). Ask students to discuss Samantha Graham's ideas in groups, then to share their views in a class discussion. Ask individuals to think about how they spent their time in the last school holidays, and to suggest one thing they might do in the next school holidays to make better use of their time.

Plenary

Ask the students to imagine that their parents have offered to give them £30 to spend over a two-week holiday period, provided that they can come up with a proposal for an activity that will be a good use of their time. Explain to a partner how they would use the money, then share some of their ideas in a class discussion.

Extension activities

Ask groups to imagine that they are members of a youth club committee and to draw up plans for a 'Summer holiday youth scheme' to run from 10.00am to 4.00pm each weekday for three weeks. Discuss the activities they would include in order to attract as many young people as possible. Then ask the groups to take turns to present the plans to the rest of the class.

Recording and evaluating

Ask students to fill in the appropriate section of Copymaster R5 to record and evaluate what they have learned from this unit.

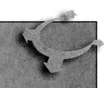

UNIT 12 You and your body – drinking and alcohol

Your Life 2/Year 8

Lesson 1 *Your Life 2*, pages 54–55
National Framework for PSHE coverage 2d, 2f

Objective: To understand the effects of drinking alcohol and to explore teenage drinking and the laws about young people and alcohol.

Resources

Copies of Copymaster 12 'How much do you know about alcohol?' (*Your Life 2 Copymasters,* page 24)

Starter

Introduce the topic with a discussion of why there is so much fuss about alcohol. Talk about how powerful a drug alcohol is and how people who get drunk often do things they later regret (e.g. get into fights, behave recklessly and cause criminal damage, have unprotected sex, drive a car and cause an accident). Talk about how alcohol can be addictive and lead to alcoholism. Stress how important it is, therefore, to know all about alcohol and what sensible drinking is.

Suggested activities

- Read about alcohol and its effects ('What's all the fuss about?', page 54) and about 'Drink strengths' (page 54). Ask the students in pairs to produce a 'True or false?' quiz based on the information in the two articles, then to give the quiz to another pair to do.

- Ask groups to discuss the statements by Kirstie and Shareen (see page 54), then to share their views in a class discussion.

- Read 'Alcohol and young people – the law' (page 55). Ask: "Should the legal age for drinking be raised, lowered, or left as it is?" Discuss the arguments for and against changing the law and/or strengthening it by increasing the penalties for people who sell alcohol to young people.

- Read 'Getting drunk' (page 55). Ask individuals to write a short statement saying what they think of people who get very drunk, then to share their views in a group discussion (see 'In groups', page 55).

Plenary

Ask: "If you were designing a poster entitled 'Think Before You Drink' to make young people aware of how drinking can affect them, what messages would you want to get across? What information would you include on the poster?" Share their ideas in a class discussion.

Extension activities

Ask individuals to draw the poster based on the ideas they discussed in the Plenary session.

Test the students' knowledge of alcohol and its effects by encouraging them to do the quiz on Copymaster 12. Then ask them to join up with a partner to check their answers by referring to the articles on these pages.

Your Life 2/Year 8

UNIT 12 You and your body – drinking and alcohol

Your Life 2/Year 8

Lesson 2 *Your Life 2*, pages 56–57
National Framework for PSHE coverage 2d, 2f

> **Objective:** To explore the problems alcohol can cause teenagers who drink too much, and to discuss how to cope with an adult in the family who has a drink problem.

Resources

Copies of Copymaster R6 'Keeping healthy' (page 186)

Starter

Recap on how people who don't regulate their drinking can become dependent on alcohol. Talk about the effect that alcoholism can have on people's lives and discuss high-profile cases of celebrities with drinking problems, e.g. George Best or Ann Robinson. Explain that you can become an alcoholic at any age if your drinking gets out of control.

Suggested activities

- Read 'Andrew's story' (page 56). Encourage groups to discuss what they learn from it about the effects drinking had on Andrew's life, about how to spot a drinking problem and how to deal with it.

- Read 'Kerry's story' (page 56). Ask: "Is she just having fun or has she got a problem?" Ask pairs to discuss and write down what they would say to Kerry to warn her of the risks of continuing to drink as much as she does. Then share their ideas in a class discussion.

- Read 'Valerie's story' (page 57). Ask groups to list all the problems Valerie has had to face because of her mother's drinking. Ask: "What do you think of the way Valerie has coped with the situation?" "What advice would you give her?"

- Invite individuals to study the advice in 'Living with someone who drinks – how to cope' (page 57), then to show their understanding of it by writing a reply to Tony's letter (see 'For your file', page 57).

Plenary

Explain that the government has considered putting health warnings on alcohol containers. Discuss how effective such warnings might be and ask students to work in pairs to draft what a warning might say on: a) a can of beer, b) a bottle of wine and c) a bottle of spirits.

Extension activity

Invite students to find more information about young people and drinking by using the internet and visiting websites such as www.wrecked.co.uk.

Recording and evaluating

Ask students to fill in the appropriate section of Copymaster R6 to record and evaluate what they have learned from this unit.

UNIT 13 You and the community – the school as a community

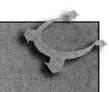

Your Life 2/Year 8

Lesson 1 *Your Life 2*, pages 58–59
National Curriculum Programme of Study for Citizenship coverage 1f, 2a, 2b, 2c; links with QCA exemplar unit 1, 17

Objective: To understand that the school is a community of different groups, and to consider how proposals for a five-term year would affect the various members of the school community.

Starter

Talk about how the school community consists of different groups and list the various groups on the board. Discuss how any major change to the organisation or routine of the school will have an impact on each of these groups. Summarise the points you have made by reading the first two paragraphs on page 58.

Suggested activities

- Read 'A new school year?' and 'School calendar shake-up' (page 58). Ensure that students understand what the proposed pattern of a five-term year is. Ask pairs to list the reasons for the proposal given in the article.

- Read the statements in 'A change for the better?' (page 59) and discuss each one in turn, encouraging the class to say whether they agree or disagree with it and why. Ask pairs to add any further reasons in favour of the proposal to their list and also to make a list of arguments against the proposal. Either organise a debate on the motion 'This house believes that a five-term year is better than a three-term year' or role play a public meeting on the issue of introducing a five-term year, in which representatives of various groups in the school community express their views.

- Ask groups to discuss how the school day is organised and to present their recommendations either for or against changing it to the rest of the class (see 'The school day', page 59).

Plenary

Explain that any changes to the school day or school year would have an impact on other groups of people, besides those in the school community, e.g. on the bus companies which supply school transport and on the catering staff who supply school meals. Discuss how they might react to the proposal for a five-term year. Stress the importance of considering every viewpoint when changes are being proposed.

Extension activity

Invite members of the different groups that make up the school community (e.g. a governor, member of the parents and teachers association, of the caretaking staff, of the administrative staff), to join a discussion of the proposal for a five-term year. Suggest the class make notes of what they say and ask them to work individually to write an article for the school newsletter reporting their views.

Your Life 2/Year 8

UNIT 13 You and the community – the school as a community

Your Life 2/Year 8

Lesson 2 *Your Life 2*, pages 60–61
National Curriculum Programme of Study for Citizenship coverage 1f, 2a, 3b;
links with QCA exemplar units 1, 14, 17

Objective: To develop skills in participation and responsible action by holding a mock election to a Year 8 council and by planning a social event.

Resources

Copies of the school's uniform regulations for Year 8

Copies of Copymaster 12A 'Understanding how to organise a social event' (page 168)

Starter

Talk about the school council (how it is composed, how members are elected, what its function is, and how information about its meetings is communicated). Ask: "How effective is it in dealing with the issues that concern Year 8 students?" Introduce the idea of having Year councils. Ask: "What are the arguments for and against having Year councils?"

Suggested activities

- Read the constitution of Beach Lane School Year 8 Council (page 60). Discuss with the class what its purpose is and how it is organised. Then hold a mock election for a Year 8 council. Invite groups to help a candidate prepare a statement to read to the rest of the class. After each candidate has spoken, hold a 'question time' in which the other members of the class can ask questions. Then hold a vote by secret ballot.

- Give groups a copy of the Year 8 dress regulations and ask them to suggest how they would like to change them. Share their ideas in a class discussion and prepare a proposal for the class representatives to put to the school council.

- Ask individuals to write a letter to the school council on a Year 8 issue (see 'For your file', page 60).

- Read 'Organising a social event' (page 61). Invite groups to choose an event and to draw up plans for it by making a list of jobs to be done, similar to the checklist given as an example (see "8L Ice-skating trip", page 61). Then allow groups, in turn, to present their proposals to the rest of the class. Hold a vote to choose one of the proposals to put forward to a Year 8 council.

Plenary

Talk about the students' proposal for a social event and vote on whether or not to take it any further.

Extension activity

If the class voted to take the proposal further, help them to appoint a planning committee and, under your guidance, allow the planning committee to organise the event. After the event, hold a discussion in which you review it (see 'Reviewing the event' page 61).

Assessment

Use Copymaster 12A to assess understanding of how to organise a social event.

UNIT 13 You and the community – the school as a community

Lesson 3 *Your Life 2*, pages 62–63
National Curriculum Programme of Study for Citizenship coverage 1f, 2a, 3b; links with QCA exemplar units 1, 14, 17

Objective: To plan and produce a Year 8 newsletter.

Resources

Copies of Copymaster 13 'Year 8 Newsletter – questionnaire' (*Your Life 2 Copymasters*, page 25)

Copies of Copymaster R8 'Developing as a citizen' (page 188)

Starter

Introduce the project by discussing with them all the tasks needed to produce the newsletter. Explain the need to set up groups to perform specific tasks, and to appoint an editorial committee to coordinate the planning and production of the newsletter. Then read the sections 'An editorial committee' on page 62.

Suggested activities

- Split the class into working groups and instruct them each to elect a representative to be on the editorial committee. Then read 'Planning the newsletter' (page 62). Ask groups to discuss who the target audience should be and the purpose of the newsletter.

- Ask: "What are its contents going to be?" Explain the importance of market research. Give students copies of Copymaster 13 to complete on their own. Then ask groups to discuss what their answers tell them about the contents people would like to see in the newsletter.

- Ask students to draft a statement of their group's proposals for the newsletter, for their representative to present to an open meeting of the editorial committee. Then encourage the editorial committee to make decisions about the purpose, target audience and contents of the newsletter.

Plenary

As a class, discuss what tasks need to be done next in order to produce the newsletter. Set a timetable for groups to do their market research and to report their findings to the editorial committee. Then set a date for publication.

Extension activities

Encourage groups to carry out further market research, using the questionnaire, to find out what other members of the school community would like to see in the newsletter. Ask groups to discuss ideas for the format of the newsletter (see 'Designing and producing the newsletter', page 63). Hold an open meeting of the editorial committee at which the representatives present their ideas and the editorial committee makes decisions.

Allow the students to write and produce the newsletter, following the guidelines on page 63.

Hold a class discussion in which you review the project and list what they would do differently if they were to produce another newsletter.

Recording and evaluating

Ask students to use the appropriate section of Copymaster R8 to help them to record and evaluate what they learned from this unit.

UNIT 14 You and your opinions – speaking your mind

Your Life 2/Year 8

 Lesson 1 *Your Life 2*, pages 64–65
National Framework for PSHE coverage 2f; National Curriculum Programme
of Study for Citizenship coverage 2a, 2b, 2c; links with QCA exemplar units
1, 14

Objective: To understand the difference between facts and opinions, to
know how to form an opinion and to practise justifying an opinion in an oral
discussion.

Resources

Copies of Copymaster 14 'Should sick children be filmed for TV programmes?'
(*Your Life 2 Copymasters,* page 26)

Copies of Copymaster 13A 'Understanding the difference between facts and
opinions' (page 169)

Starter

Explain that while listening to an argument we need to be able to distinguish
between a fact, which is a true statement, and an opinion, which is a judgement or
belief. Read 'Facts and opinions' (page 64) and make sure everyone understands
the difference between a fact and an opinion.

Suggested activities

- Ask pairs to study the list of ten statements (see 'In pairs', page 64) and decide
  which are facts and which are opinions.

- Talk about how, if we are going to discuss an issue, we need to research it to
  find out the facts and what the different opinions on it are. Read 'Forming your
  opinion' (page 64). Teach the students the mnemonic FIDO to help them
  remember how to form an opinion: Find out the Facts, Identify the Issues,
  Decide your Opinion.

- Ask individuals to study all the information and views on body-piercing ('Should
  body-piercing be banned?', page 65), to make notes on the facts and opinions
  they contain, and to form their own opinion on body-piercing. Then allow them
  to share their views in groups.

- Ask individuals to write a short statement expressing their opinions on body-
  piercing (see 'For your file', page 65).

Plenary

Ask some students to read their statements and discuss how clearly they stated
their arguments and whether or not they used facts to support their opinions.

Extension activity

Ask individuals to study Copymaster 14, to form their own opinions on the issue,
then to share their views in a group discussion.

Assessment

Use Copymaster 13A to assess understanding of the difference between facts and
opinions.

Answers: 1. opinion, 2. fact, 3. opinion, 4. fact, 5. fact, 6. opinion, 7. opinion,
8. fact, 9. fact, 10. opinion.

 Your Life 2/Year 8

UNIT 14 You and your opinions – speaking your mind

Lesson 2 *Your Life 2*, pages 66–67
National Curriculum Programme of Study for Citizenship coverage 2a, 2b, 2c

Objective: To understand the rules of debating, to explore techniques that can be used to make speeches effective and to participate in a debate.

Resources

Copies of Copymaster R8 'Developing as a citizen' (page 188)

Starter

Explain the difference between an informal discussion, which does not follow a set pattern dictated by rules, and a formal debate, which has a set pattern of rules. Talk about why there are rules in formal debates, and how they allow people to express their arguments without being interrupted and to hear and consider different opinions.

Suggested activities

- Read and explain 'The rules of debating' (page 66). Ask students, in groups, to compile a glossary of debating terms to put in their files.

- Plan a debate to take place in a follow-up lesson. Invite students either to suggest a motion themselves or to choose one of the three motions from page 66 (see 'Organise your own debate') and write the motion on the board.

- Explain that you are going to split the class into two groups; ask one group to prepare speeches for the motion and the other to prepare speeches against. Before they begin, read and discuss 'Tips on writing a speech' (page 67). Then allow them to start planning their speeches in pairs, by discussing where they can find out more about the issue and listing the main arguments for and against the motion.

Plenary

Hold a class discussion in which you talk about the arguments they have identified. List the arguments for and against the motion on the board and ask the students to copy them to refer to as they plan their speeches. Discuss how they can research the issue to find out more information on it.

Extension activities

Ask the students to write their speeches and hand them in. Then choose people to act as proposer and seconder, and opposer and seconder, and hold the debate.

Review how the debate went. Talk about whose speeches were most effective, and why.

Recording and evaluation

Ask students to use the appropriate section of Copymaster R8 to help them to record and evaluate what they learned from this lesson.

UNIT 15 You and your body – contraception and safer sex

Your Life 2/Year 8

Lesson 1 *Your Life 2*, pages 68–69
National Framework for PSHE coverage 2e

> **Objective:** To provide information on contraception and safer sex, and to examine the steps that can be taken to avoid unwanted pregnancies and protection against STIs.

Resources

Leaflets for teenagers, obtainable from family planning clinics, giving factual information about contraception and STIs (optional)

Starter

Explain what is meant by 'the age of consent' and why there is a legal age of consent. Talk about how it aims to protect young people and how anyone who decides to have sex before the age of consent is taking a risk. Discuss how a boy can be prosecuted for having sex with an under-age girl and how the girl is taking a risk of getting pregnant. There is also the risk of catching a sexually transmitted infection. Explain that it is important to think carefully before having sex, and to know what safer sex is and how to practise it.

Suggested activities

- Read 'Sex and contraception … your questions answered' (page 68). Hold a class discussion in which you ask whether they have any comments to make on the advice that is given or questions to ask about it.

- Read 'Natural methods of preventing unwanted pregnancies' (page 69). Discuss why the rhythm method is unsuitable for teenagers and why withdrawal is unreliable.

- Read 'I'm worried about protection' (page 69). Discuss the reasons Tricia Kreitman gives for advising the 13-year-old girl not to have sex with her boyfriend. Ask: "Do you agree with Tricia Kreitman? Why?"

- Read 'How can I avoid AIDS?' on page 69. Discuss what they learn about a) how AIDS is caught? and b) how to avoid catching AIDS.

Plenary

In a class discussion, talk about what the students have learned from this lesson about safer sex: a) about how to avoid an unwanted pregnancy and b) about how to avoid AIDS.

Extension activity

In groups, discuss the arguments for and against either raising or lowering the age of consent (see 'In groups', page 69). Then share their views in a class discussion.

Read the leaflets on methods of contraception and how to avoid catching STIs and discuss the information and advice they give.

UNIT 15 You and your body – contraception and safer sex

Your Life 2/Year 8

Lesson 2 *Your Life 2*, pages 70–71
National Framework for PSHE coverage 2e

Objective: To explain the rights and responsibilities that a person has in any sexual relationship and to examine common myths about having sex.

Resources

Copies of Copymaster 15 'Sex facts and fictions' (*Your Life 2 Copymasters*, page 27)

Copies of Copymaster R6 'Keeping healthy' (page 186)

Starter

Explain that in any relationship you have rights and responsibilities. It is your *right* to be able to do only the things you want to do and to refuse to do things you do not want to do. It is your *responsibility* to respect the rights of other people and not to try to pressurise or force them to do things they do not want to do.

Suggested activities

- Read about sexual rights and responsibilities (page 70). Ask groups to discuss what they consider to be the most important points made in the article. Then encourage them to share their ideas in a class discussion.

- Ask individuals to study the list of types of behaviour (see 'What is acceptable in a sexual relationship?', page 71), and to write down which they consider to be acceptable and unacceptable or are not sure about. Then allow them to share their views in a group discussion, followed by a class discussion.

- Read 'Sex myths' (page 71). Then in groups draft a reply to this letter:

  Dear Erica,

  My boyfriend is pressurising me to have sex, but I'm not sure. He says everyone is doing it and that it will bring us closer. When I tried to talk about taking precautions, he said he'd leave me to sort them out. I'm confused. What should I do?

  Josie

Plenary

Encourage students to share their replies to Josie's letter in a class discussion, drawing attention to the points they make about Josie's rights and responsibilities. Conclude the lesson by rereading the articles on page 70.

Extension activities

Use Copymaster 15 to check students' knowledge and understanding. Read out the statements and ask them on their own to write down whether or not the statement is fact or fiction. Then hand out the sheet and ask them to check their answers, reading and discussing the explanations under each statement.

Recording and evaluating

Ask students to fill in the appropriate section of Copymaster R6 to record and evaluate what they have learned from this unit.

Your Life 2/Year 8

UNIT 16 You as a citizen – of the European Union

Your Life 2/Year 8

Lesson 1 *Your Life 2*, pages 72–73
National Curriculum Programme of Study for Citizenship coverage 1i, 2a, 2b, 2c; links with QCA exemplar unit 1

> **Objective:** To explain how the European Union developed and to examine Britain's relationship with the EU.

Starter

Explain how until the middle of the 20th century the history of Europe was a story of wars between nation states. In the Middle Ages there was the Hundred Years War between England and France, in Tudor Times England and Spain were at war, at the start of the 19th century there were the Napoleonic wars and then in the 20th century there were the two world wars. It is only in the last 50 years that the idea of Europe as a community of states with common interests has taken hold and states have joined together to form the European Union.

Look at the map on page 72 and discuss how, with only a few exceptions (Norway, Switzerland and the states that were formerly Yugoslavia), the states of Europe are members of the EU.

Suggested activities

- Read 'How it began' (page 72). Invite pairs to make notes on when and why the EEC was formed, and why Britain did not join until 1973. Then hold a class discussion about the formation of the EEC and the reasons why it was not until 1973 that Britain became a member.

- Read 'The development of the EU' (page 72) and ask the students to draw a time-line from 1951 to 2004 to show the important events in the development of the EU.

- Explain what customs duties are and how you may have to pay taxes on goods bought in another country. Then read 'The single market' (page 73). Explain what the single market is and discuss what the advantages are for the EU countries that are part of it.

- Read 'Should Britain remain in the EU?' (page 73). Ask pairs to identify and list the arguments for and against Britain's membership of the EU. Then hold a class discussion in which students share their views on whether or not Britain should stay in the EU.

Plenary

Give the class a quick quiz on the information they have learned in the lesson. You could organise it as a 'True or false?' quiz with questions such as: 'The EU used to be known as the ECU or European Customs Union – true or false?'

Extension activity

Hold a formal debate on the motion 'This house believes that Britain should withdraw from the EU'.

UNIT 16 You as a citizen – of the European Union

Lesson 2 *Your Life 2*, pages 74–75
National Curriculum Programme of Study for Citizenship coverage 1i, 2a, 2b, 2c; links with QCA exemplar unit 1

Objective: To understand how being a citizen of the EU affects your life and to examine what the EU does to protect the environment.

Starter

Explain that anyone who is a British citizen is also a citizen of the European Union. Explain that this means we have rights and responsibilities under European law as well as UK law. People over 18 vote to elect the European Parliament and a proportion of the taxes we pay goes to the European Union. Explain that being citizens of the EU affects our lives in many ways.

Suggested activities

- Read 'How does the EU affect you?' (page 74). Ask the students to study the article in pairs. They should then imagine they have to condense the article so that it answers the question "What does the EU do for you?" in not more than 150 words. What are the key points they would make? Allow them to draft their condensed versions, then to read them out and compare them in a group or class discussion. **AO**

- Read 'What is being done by the EU to protect the environment?' (page 75). Ask groups to study the article and to list all the measures that the EU has taken so far to protect the environment. Can they suggest any others that could be added? Encourage them to share their views in a class discussion.

- Ask groups to imagine they are members of a Green Party working on a speech to be made by a Green candidate standing in a European election. Ask them to work together on ideas for the speech, stating why they think protecting the environment is so important, explaining what the EU has done already and what more they think needs to be done. Then ask them to work alone and draft the candidate's statement (see 'For your file', page 75).

Plenary

Ask students to imagine that a European election is about to take place. They meet someone who expresses the view: "Why should I vote? What does the EU do for me?" Hold a class discussion on what they would say the EU does for him or her and how they would try to persuade him or her to vote.

UNIT 16 You as a citizen – of the European Union

Your Life 2/Year 8

Lesson 3 *Your Life 2*, pages 76–77
National Curriculum Programme of Study for Citizenship coverage 1i, 2a, 2b, 2c; links with QCA exemplar unit 1

> **Objective:** To explain the institutions which run the European Union, and to learn how European laws are made and how the EU is financed.

Starter

Explain what an institution is (an organisation set up for a specific purpose) and that the focus of the lesson is on the institutions that have been set up to run the European Union. Talk about how each of the member nation states of the European Union is a democracy (a country in which all the citizens share power by electing representatives to make decisions on their behalf). Explain that the European Union is a democratic community of states and its institutions are democratic institutions.

Suggested activities

- Read 'European institutions' (page 76). Ask pairs to make notes on the five main institutions, using the headings 'Composition' and 'Functions' for each institution. Then, as a class, discuss each institution in turn, focusing on what they have learned about its composition, where it is based and what its functions are.

- Read 'How European laws are made' (page 77). Hold a class discussion about the different roles in the law-making process played by the European Commission, the European Parliament and the Council of the European Union. Ask the students to make a copy of the flowchart for their files.

- Read 'The EU budget' (page 77). Talk about how the EU budget is set, how the EU raises money and how it spends it. Then ask groups to discuss their views on whether they think it is right for rich countries to contribute more in order to help poorer countries to develop their economies.

Plenary

Ask pairs to compile a glossary of terms about the organisation of the European Union.

Extension activity

Ask individuals to find out more about the European Union's institutions from the internet by visiting sites such as the European Parliament's website (www.europarl.eu.int).

UNIT 16 You as a citizen – of the European Union

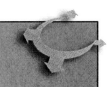

Your Life 2/Year 8

Lesson 4 *Your Life 2*, pages 78–79
National Curriculum Programme of Study for Citizenship coverage 1i, 2a, 2b, 2c; links with QCA exemplar unit 1

Objective: To explore issues concerning the future development of the EU, to explain what the single currency is and to discuss whether Britain should join it.

Resources

Copies of Copymaster 16 'How much do you know about the EU?' (*Your Life 2 Copymasters*, page 28)

Copies of Copymaster 14A 'Understanding the European Union' (page 170)

Copies of Copymaster R8 'Developing as a citizen' (page 188)

Starter

Explain that the EU is still developing as an organisation. One key change recently taken is the admission of ten new countries. Explain that to become a member a country has to meet certain requirements, reading page 78 to discuss those requirements.

Suggested activities

- Read 'Enlargement' (page 78). Ask students to work in pairs and to note down what the article says are the arguments for and against the increased size of the EU. Then in groups discuss the view that any country that meets the requirements and applies for membership should automatically be admitted. Explain what is meant by the term 'a federal Europe' then read 'Towards a Federal Europe?' (page 78). Draw two columns on the board labeled 'For' and 'Against'. List the arguments for and against the countries in the EU developing closer political links. Encourage students to share their views in a class discussion.

- Explain what is meant by the term 'currency' and how, in the past, the countries in the EU all had separate currencies. Then read the three paragraphs about how the euro was introduced ('The single currency', page 79). Read 'Should Britain join the euro?' (page 79). Ask groups to discuss their views, then debate the question with the class and hold a vote on the issue.

Plenary

Ask each student to write a sentence saying why they are in favour of or opposed to the further development of the EU by enlarging it or developing closer political links between its members. Ask some to read their statements to the class.

Extension activity

Test the students' knowledge of the European Union using Copymaster 6.

A0

Assessment

Use Copymaster 14A to assess knowledge of the European Union.

Answers: Across – 1. Rome, 3. trade, 5. Euro, 6. Finland, 9. Strasbourg, 12. net, 13. six, 14. council, 15. Spain. Down – 1. referendum, 2. ministers, 3. ten, 4. out, 7. court, 8. blue flag, 10. Greece, 11. taxes.

Recording and evaluating

Ask students to use the appropriate section of Copymaster R8 to record and evaluate what they learned from this unit.

UNIT 17 You and the community – taking action on the local environment

Your Life 2/Year 8

Lesson 1 *Your Life 2*, page 80
National Curriculum Programme of Study for Citizenship coverage 1f, 2a, 3b; links with QCA exemplar unit 18

Objective: To investigate the condition of the school environment and to develop plans for improving it.

Starter

Ask the students: "Whose responsibility is it to take care of the school environment?" Discuss their responses, then ask them to read and discuss the six quotations at the top of page 80. Talk about how much the school environment matters, why some people are prepared to put up with things at school which they wouldn't tolerate at home, and about how looking after the environment is the responsibility of all the different members of the school community.

Suggested activities

- Ask the students to work individually to carry out a survey of the condition of the school's buildings and grounds (see 'An environmental survey', page 80). Then ask groups to discuss their assessments of the condition of the different areas of the school and to choose three areas as priority areas for improvement. Share the groups' views in a class discussion and select one priority for the class representative to raise as an issue at the next meeting of the school council.

- Encourage groups to discuss what proposal they would put forward as a bid for £25,000 of lottery money, if it was available for a project to improve the school's environment. Make a list of different ideas, then choose one and draft a detailed proposal to put to the rest of the class. Invite the class to debate the proposals and vote to choose the proposal that has the most support.

- Ask groups to discuss what could be done to improve the appearance and atmosphere of the tutor group room and to prepare a five-point plan to improve it and keep it in good condition. Then share the students' ideas in a class discussion and agree a class five-point plan.

Plenary

Remind the students that for the school environment to be kept in a good condition then they must behave responsibly towards it. In a class discussion, draw up a list of guidelines ('Dos' and 'Don'ts') in order to respect and protect the school environment.

Extension activity

Put into action the class's five-point plan to improve the tutor group room (see point 3 of 'In groups', page 80).

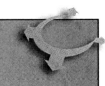

UNIT 17 You and the community – taking action on the local environment

Your Life 2/Year 8

Lesson 2 *Your Life 2*, pages 81–83
National Curriculum Programme of Study for Citizenship coverage 1c, 2a, 3b, 3c; links with QCA exemplar unit 7

Objective: To understand what Local Agenda 21 is and what sustainable development is, to investigate how the local environment might be improved and to participate in a project to help the local community.

Resources

Copies of Copymaster 17 'Help protect your environment' (*Your Life 2 Copymasters*, page 29)

Copies of Copymaster 15A 'Understanding Local Agenda 21' (page 171)

Copies of Copymaster R8 'Developing as a citizen' (page 188)

Starter

Read the introductory paragraph about the environment on page 81. Ask students to work on their own to make lists of things we can all do in our daily lives to save energy, to cut down waste and reduce pollution. Hold a class discussion.

Suggested activities

- Read and discuss 'Changing the way we live' (page 81). Then ask students to produce a poster designed to get young people to lead a sustainable lifestyle, entitled 'Your Environment Needs YOU!'

- Read the information about how young people have become involved in Groundwork's activities (pages 82–83). Encourage groups to discuss how the local environment in the area nearby can be improved. Encourage them to share their ideas in a class discussion and to write a letter to the local newspaper saying what they think needs to be done.

- Read 'Go MADD' (page 83). Ask groups to draft a proposal for a MADD event to take place over two to three hours one evening after school or on a Saturday morning. Ask them to list activities that could help the local community.

Plenary

Encourage students to share their ideas for a MADD event in a class discussion and decide which activities to include in the event. Draw up a plan and list everything that needs to be done to organise the event.

Extension activities

Hold the MADD event. Suggest students draft a press release to send to local newspapers, either before the event saying what they plan to do or after the event reporting what they did. Students then complete Copymaster 17.

Assessment

Use Copymaster 15A to assess understanding of Local Agenda 21.

Answers: 1. pollution, 2. councils, 3. recycling, 4. sustainable, 5. development, 6. waste, 7. energy, 8. resources, 9. environment, 10. reduce, 11. earth.

Recording and evaluation

Ask students to use the appropriate section of Copymaster R8 to record and evaluate what they learned from this unit.

Your Life 2/Year 8

UNIT 18 You and other people – older people

Your Life 2/Year 8

Lesson 1 *Your Life 2*, pages 84–85
National Framework for PSHE coverage 3a, 3b; National Curriculum
Programme of Study for Citizenship coverage 2a, 2b, 2c, 3a

Objective: To explore attitudes towards older people and what is meant by ageism, and to examine the problems some older people face.

Resources

Copies of Copymaster 18 'Older people and their homes' (*Your Life 2 Copymasters*, page 30)

Starter

Ask students, in pairs, to brainstorm all the words and phrases they associate with old age and older people. Then ask them to decide whether, overall, they have a positive or negative view of old age and older people. Encourage them to share their views in a class discussion. Remind them of what a stereotype is and ask: "Is your view of older people based on a stereotype?"

Suggested activities

- Read the article 'Ageism' (page 84). Ask groups to discuss what it says about attitudes to older people and how older people are presented in the media. Then ask them to read '82 year old forced to give up job' (page 84), and to discuss whether society undervalues older people. Encourage them to talk about older people they know and how they spend their time.

- Read 'Survey finds "two worlds of old age"' (page 85). Ask groups to discuss the survey's findings, talking about the factors that determine what sort of life an older person leads, and what they learn from the survey about the problems some older people face. Then focus on memory loss and read 'Old age and memory loss' (page 84). Ask pairs to identify and list the key facts about dementia that they learn from the article.

- Read 'Caring for older people' (page 85) and ask groups to discuss the issues raised in the questions in 'What role should the family play?' Encourage them to share their ideas in a class discussion.

Plenary

Invite the class to imagine they are working on a magazine that is going to feature an article on 'Myths about older people'. Write the headings 'Facts' and 'Fictions' on the board and make a list of the facts and fictions that the students would include in the article.

Extension activities

Invite pairs or groups to study the letter on Copymaster 18 and to draft a reply to it.

Ask the students to show their understanding of ageism by planning and writing an article on the causes and effects of ageism (see 'For your file', page 84).

Suggest individuals find more information about older people from the internet, such as the Age Concern website www.ace.org.uk.

UNIT 18 You and other people – older people

Your Life 2/Year 8

Lesson 2 *Your Life 2*, pages 86–87
National Framework for PSHE coverage 3a, 3b; National Curriculum
Programme of Study for Citizenship coverage 2a, 2b, 2c, 3a

Objective: To understand how the age profile of society is changing, and to consider the implications of an increase in the number of older people in the future.

Resources

Copies of Copymaster R7 'Developing relationships' (page 187)

Starter

Ask the students: "How do you see yourself in 60 years time?" "What sort of life will most of you have as you grow older?" "Will you be fitter and healthier than the older people of today?" "Will you still be able to retire and claim a pension at 60 or 65, or will you have to go working?" "Will you still get free healthcare or will it be rationed?" "Will you face a comfortable or a bleak old age?" Ask them to jot down their ideas on what they think life will be like for older people in 2070 and share them in a class discussion.

Suggested activities

- Explain that the age profile of society is changing. Read and discuss 'Forecasts for the future' (page 86). Then read 'How will life be different in the 21st century?' (page 86). Ask groups to discuss the questions raised in the last three paragraphs.

- Ask groups to study the picture and caption on page 86, then discuss the questions about rationing and the provision of healthcare (see 'In groups', page 86). Challenge them to prepare a statement on their views of 'How to provide health care in the 21st century'. Encourage them to share their views in a class discussion.

- Read and discuss in groups the questions raised in the three life stories on page 87.

Plenary

Summarise what the students have been discussing by making a list of the changes that they think will result from the change in the age profile of society. Discuss which of the changes they think will have the most impact on their life.

Recording and evaluating

Ask students to fill in the appropriate section of Copymaster R7 to record and evaluate what they have learned from this unit.

UNIT 19 You and global issues – food and water

Your Life 2/Year 8

Lesson 1 *Your Life 2*, pages 88–89
National Curriculum Programme of Study for Citizenship coverage 1i, 2a, 2b, 2c; links with QCA exemplar unit 10

> **Objective:** To explore concerns about how our foods are produced, and to debate the arguments for and against genetically modified foods.

Resources

Copies of Copymaster 19 'Genetically modified foods – for and against' (*Your Life 2 Copymasters*, page 31)

Starter

Talk about what we do when we're shopping for food. Ask: "What influences your choice of one product rather than another – is it the taste, the price, the look of the products, an advertisement you've seen or someone's recommendation?" Discuss what influences us. Then ask: "Do you ever try to find out more about food before you buy it – such as where it came from, how it was produced or what exactly is in it? Ask: "How important do you think such questions are?" Explain that they may be more important than they think, as the article they are going to study will explain.

Suggested activities

- Read the article 'The foods you eat' (pages 88–89), stopping after each section to discuss the points made. Then invite students to write answers to questions 1–4 on page 89, then to share their views in a group or class discussion.

- Ask individuals to show their understanding of the article by writing a letter to a newspaper expressing their views on one or more of the issues raised in the article (see 'For your file', page 89).

Plenary

Encourage students to share views they have expressed in their letters in a class discussion.

Extension activities

Ask groups to study Copymaster 19, listing the key points made by the writers. Challenge them to research the issue further on the internet, then to draft speeches for a debate on the motion 'This house believes that the benefits of GM foods outweigh the risks'.

Ask students to find out about the True Food Campaign, organised by Greenpeace to make people aware of what environmentalists regard as the true cost of food, by visiting the website www.truefood.org.

UNIT 19 You and global issues – food and water

Your Life 2/Year 8

Lesson 2 *Your Life 2*, pages 90–91
National Curriculum Programme of Study for Citizenship coverage 1i, 2a, 2b, 2c, 3a; links with QCA exemplar unit 10

Objective: To examine the causes of food shortages and famine and to explore ways of solving the problem of world hunger.

Resources

Copies of Copymaster 16A 'Understanding world hunger' (page 172)

Starter

Explain what is meant by malnutrition and note that there are two main causes: 1) not getting enough food; 2) not getting enough of different foods to give all the nutrients the body needs. Explain that there are three main types of malnutrition: 1) protein energy malnutrition, due to a lack of protein and carbohydrate, which causes two illnesses in children (marasmus and kwashiorkor) both of which can be fatal; 2) vitamin deficiency caused by not having enough fruit and vegetables, which can cause beri beri and rickets; 3) mineral deficiency, e.g. lack of iron which can cause anaemia. Then read the first paragraph on page 90.

Suggested activities

- Explain what a famine is (an extreme shortage of food in one place). Read 'The causes of food shortages and famine' (page 90) stopping after each paragraph to discuss each piece of information in turn. Then read and discuss the paragraph on 'Overpopulation' (page 91) before asking students to work individually to make a list of the key points they have learned from the articles.

- Read 'Unequal shares' (page 91), then invite groups to study the list of ten reasons people give for why there is hunger in Sub-Saharan Africa, and to discuss which are true. Encourage students to share their views in a class discussion.

- Ask individuals to study 'Ten ways to beat world hunger' and to rank the ideas in order of importance.

Plenary

Invite students to share their views of the ten suggestions for beating world hunger in a class discussion. Ask: "Which of the suggestions would be most likely to have a long-term effect?"

Extension activities

Ask individuals to write a statement expressing their thoughts about the issue of world hunger. In addition to drawing on the information from these pages, suggest they research further information on websites such as the Oxfam Cool Planet website www.oxfam.org.uk/coolplanet/.

Assessment

Use Copymaster 16A to assess understanding of the reasons for world hunger.

Your Life 2/Year 8

UNIT 19 You and global issues – food and water

Your Life 2/Year 8

Lesson 3 *Your Life 2*, pages 92–93
National Curriculum Programme of Study for Citizenship coverage 1i, 2a, 2b, 2c, 3a; links with QCA exemplar unit 10

Objective: To understand that there is a shortage of water in many parts of the world and to explore how this affects people's lives.

Resources

Copies of Copymaster R8 'Developing as a citizen' (page 188)

Starter

Ask the students to list all the different ways in which we use water in our homes. Then discuss how different their lives would be if their home wasn't connected to a water supply. Ask: "What if you had to walk four to five kilometres to get your water from a well or a standpipe?" "What if you had to spend a quarter of your income on clean water because all the rivers around you were polluted with sewage?" Explain that this is what many people in the world have to do, and what people in the UK had to do only 100 years ago. Then read 'Life in the cities' and 'Women and water' (page 93).

Suggested activities

- Read 'The water crisis'. Write these questions on the board and ask individuals to write answers to them: 1) Explain what people mean when they say there is a water crisis. 2) Why is there a water crisis? 3) What problems result from the lack of fresh clean water? 4) How can these problems be solved? Then invite pairs to mark each other's answers as you discuss the answers with the class. **AO**

- Ask individuals to do the quiz 'How much do you know about water?' (page 92) and discuss the answers in a class discussion.

- Read 'Water wars' (page 93). Explain how water is required not only in homes but for industry and agriculture. Ask: "How serious a threat to world peace do you think the water crisis is: very, quite or not **very**?"

- Ask students to imagine they work for a charity called The Freshwater Fund which supports schemes to provide people in other parts of the world with fresh clean water. Challenge groups to plan a 30-second TV advert asking people to donate £3 a month to the charity.

Plenary

Encourage the students to share their ideas for the TV advert. Discuss the key information that each of their adverts tries to put across, and ask them to decide which group's advert would be the most effective and why.

Extension activity

Ask students to find out more information about water issues, by visiting websites of organisations such as Water Aid (www.wateraid.org.uk).

Recording and evaluating

Ask students to use the appropriate section of Copymaster R8 to help them to record and evaluate what they have learned from this unit.

UNIT 20 You and your achievements – recording your progress

Your Life 2/Year 8

Lesson *Your Life 2*, pages 94–95
National Framework for PSHE coverage 1a; National Curriculum Programme
of Study for Citizenship coverage 3c; links with QCA exemplar unit 19

> **Objective:** To review your progress and achievements in Year 8 and to
> draw up an action plan setting targets for Year 9.

Resources

Copies of Copymaster 20 'Action plans' (*Your Life 2 Copymasters*, page 32)

Copies of Copymaster R5 'Understanding yourself' (page 185)

Starter

Explain that the lesson is the start of a four-step process: 1) Thinking about your
progress and achievements; 2) Discussing your progress and achievements with
your tutor and identifying targets for Year 9; 3) Writing a statement for your
Record of Achievement; 4) Drawing up an action plan which sets targets and plans
for achieving them.

Suggested activities

- Read 'Your subjects' (page 94) and ask the students to use the five-point scale
  to give themselves grades, before writing a statement about their progress in
  each subject.

- Read 'Your key skills' (page 94) and invite the students to write a statement
  reviewing their progress in each of the key skills.

- Read 'Your activities' (page 94) and challenge the students to write a statement
  about their most significant achievements during the year.

- Read "Your attitude and behaviour" (page 94) and suggest they write a
  statement summing up their attitude and behaviour during the year.

Plenary

Allocate times for individuals to meet with you to discuss their statements and
identify targets, allowing them further time (as necessary) to complete their
statements.

Extension activities

Hold the discussion meetings with individuals. During the discussion, ask them to
note down any points you make (see 'Discussing your progress', page 95).

Ask students to write a statement to put into their Record of Achievement (see
'Recording your achievements', page 95).

Read 'Setting targets' and 'Making an action plan' (page 95). Give the students
copies of Copymaster 20 to fill in their targets for Year 9 and details of how they
plan to achieve them.

Recording and evaluating

Ask students to fill in the appropriate section of Copymaster R5 to record and
evaluate what they learned in this unit.

UNIT 1 You and your body – adolescence

Your Life 3/Year 9

Lesson 1 *Your Life 3*, pages 6–7
National Framework for PSHE coverage 1a, 1c

> **Objective:** To develop a sense of identity by thinking about what sort of person you are, your values and ambitions and what image of yourself you want to give others.

Starter

Read the introductory paragraph and the section on 'You and your identity' (page 6). Ask the students each to think about what sort of person they are, to tell a partner and to see if the partner agrees with them. Then read and discuss 'Your values and beliefs' (page 6). Discuss the viewpoint that it's always better for friends to agree to disagree than for one of them to do something they don't believe is right.

Suggested activities

- Ask the students to study the list of characteristics (see box on page 6), decide which ones their ideal person would have and then rank them in order of importance. Encourage the students to share their ideas in a group discussion.

- Read 'Your goals and ambitions' (page 6) and prompt individuals to write a short statement saying how they see themselves in ten years' time, and what they hope to have achieved by then. Invite them to share what they have written, but only if they wish to do so.

- Read the introductory paragraphs and the article 'You and your image' (page 7). Ask groups to discuss each piece of advice that Jane Goldman gives and to say why they agree or disagree with it. Encourage them to share their views in a class discussion.

Plenary

Conclude the lesson with a class discussion of characteristics the students admire and ask who their role model is. Suggest they write down the name of someone whom they would choose as their role model, and then to explain why they chose that person.

Extension activities

Ask students to bring in pictures or posters of people they admire, to write comments saying why they admire them, and to make a wall display entitled 'People we admire'.

Ask students to write an article for a teenage magazine's 'In my opinion' column, expressing their ideas about fashion, the pressures that are put on teenagers to be fashionable and how to cope with such pressures.

UNIT 1 You and your body – adolescence

Your Life 3/Year 9

Lesson 2 *Your Life 3*, pages 8–9
National Framework for PSHE coverage 1d, 2a, 2c, 3e

> **Objective:** To develop an understanding of emotions, exploring how to cope with mood swings and how to deal with anger and frustration.

Resources

Copies of Copymaster 1 'Don't bottle it up' (*Your Life 3 Copymasters*, page 13)

Copies of Copymaster R10 'Keeping healthy' (page 190)

Starter

Explain that an important part of being an adult is learning to recognise your feelings, what is creating them and how to deal with them. So it's useful, if you can, to identify what triggers your feelings. Ask individuals to think of three things that put them in a good mood (e.g. listening to their favourite music, being with their friends, playing sport, enjoying their hobby) and three things that put them in a bad mood (e.g. getting told off by a parent, not being allowed to do something, being made fun of by a friend). List on the board examples of the positive things that make them feel good and the negative things that make them feel bad. Explain that understanding what makes you feel bad and how you can make yourself feel good is important in learning how to handle your emotions.

Suggested activities

- Explain that identifying the causes of your feelings is not always simple. Read and discuss 'Mood swings' (page 8). Ask groups to study the list of problems and discuss who is the best person to talk to in each case. Encourage them to share their views in a class discussion.

- Read 'Coping with your moods' (page 9). Discuss with the class the advice it gives about how to identify the cause of a bad mood and about the positive actions they can take to deal with it, and how to avoid a repetition of it. Ask willing individuals to share personal experiences of successfully coping with a bad mood.

- Read 'Difficult feelings – anger' (page 8) and 'Difficult feelings – frustration' (page 9). Invite groups to discuss the advice given, to identify what they consider to be the most useful points and to share their views in a class discussion.

Plenary

Read Dave's letter (see 'For your file', page 9) and list the main points they would make in reply. If time allows, allow pairs or groups to draft a reply.

Extension activities

Read 'I can't take any more' on Copymaster 1, and ask groups to discuss the questions in groups, before sharing their views in a class discussion. Ask pairs to discuss Jem's problem, and test the students' understanding of how to deal with negative feelings by asking them to draft Tina's reply to Jem.

Recording and evaluating

Ask students to fill in the appropriate section of Copymaster R10 to record and evaluate what they have learned from this unit.

Your Life 3/Year 9

UNIT 2 You and your responsibilities – racism, prejudice and discrimination

Your Life 3/Year 9

Lesson 1 *Your Life 3*, pages 10–11
National Framework for PSHE coverage 3a, 3b, 3j; National Curriculum Programme of Study for Citizenship coverage 1b, 2a; links with QCA exemplar unit 4

Objective: To understand what racism is and to explore why some people are racist.

Resources

Copies of Copymaster 2 'Talking about race' (*Your Life 3 Copymasters*, page 14)

Starter

Write the terms 'racism', 'prejudice' and 'discrimination' on the board. Challenge pairs to draft definitions of them and then to check the accuracy of their definitions by reading 'What is racism?' (page 10). Explain the meaning of the terms 'stereotyping' (the belief that people from one group share the same characteristics) and 'harassment' (troubling someone by persistently attacking, insulting or abusing them). Explain what 'persecution' means (unfair and cruel treatment of a person), and that racial discrimination is a form of persecution.

Suggested activities

- Read 'Racism is …' (page 10). Ask groups to discuss what racism means to each of the five teenagers. Give them a large sheet of paper to write down what types of behaviour they regard as racist, e.g. singing chants about black players at football matches, poking fun at the way people dress, and refusing to consider someone for a job because of their race. Encourage them to share their views in a class discussion and to discuss why racist jokes are unacceptable.

- Read 'Why are some people racist?' (page 11). As a class, discuss what it tells them about the roots of racism and the human suffering that has resulted from persecution based on racist beliefs. Ask: "How has genetic science proved that the idea of superior and inferior races is false?"

- Read 'Racists – what's their problem?' (page 11). Encourage groups to discuss the reasons it suggests for why people are racists, and to add any other reasons, e.g. ignorance (they still believe in the idea of superior and inferior races), jealousy (they are jealous when people from ethnic minorities succeed and they don't). In a class discussion, ask: "What do you think is the main reason why some people in Britain today are racist?"

Plenary

Explain that it has been suggested that education is the key to getting rid of racism. Discuss with the students what they have learned about racism, what racist behaviour is and why some people are racist. Do they agree that education is the key to getting rid of racism?

Extension activity

Read Copymaster 2 and hold a class discussion of what it says about the terms people use. Ask whether they agree with the views it expresses about which terms are acceptable and which are unacceptable.

UNIT 2 You and your responsibilities – racism, prejudice and discrimination

Your Life 3/Year 9

Lesson 2 *Your Life 3*, pages 12–13
National Framework for PSHE coverage 3a, 3b, 3j; National Curriculum
Programme of Study for Citizenship coverage 1b, 2a, 3a; links with QCA
exemplar unit 4

Objective: To examine racial discrimination, exploring what it feels like to be a victim, how widespread it is and what is meant by institutional racism.

Starter

Remind students of the list of types of racist behaviour that they drew up in the last lesson, referring to what they wrote on their large sheets of paper. Ask: "What are the consequences of racist behaviour?" Talk about how racial attacks can lead to deaths, as in the cases of Stephen Lawrence and Damilola Taylor, how families can be driven from their homes by constant harassment, and how young people's lives can be made a misery by racial bullying. Explain that in the first part of the lesson you are going to be looking at what it feels like to be a victim of racism.

Suggested activities

- Read 'Victims of racism' (page 12). Invite groups to discuss what they learn from the stories about what it feels like to be a victim of racism. Then ask individuals to write a story, a poem or a playscript about a person who is a victim of racism, showing the person's feelings.

- Read 'How much discrimination is there?' (page 13). Suggest pairs make notes on what they learn from it about racial discrimination in the UK today, which groups are the main victims, and what the statistics show on how widespread it is. Then ask them to share what they have learned about discrimination in a group discussion.

- Introduce students to the term 'institutional racism', discussing the quotations on page 13 to help explain its meaning. Then read 'Racism "rife in justice system"' (page 13) and discuss the effects of racism in the criminal justice system.

Plenary

Ask students to think about their experiences and what they have discussed in the lesson. Ask: "How serious a problem do you think racism is?" Challenge them to share their views with the rest of the class.

Extension activity

Encourage pairs to role play a scene in which someone who has been the victim of either racial harassment or racial abuse tells a friend what happened and how they feel about it (see 'Role play', page 12).

UNIT 2 You and your responsibilities – racism, prejudice and discrimination

Your Life 3/Year 9

Lesson 3 *Your Life 3*, pages 14–15
National Framework for PSHE coverage 3a, 3b, 3j, 3k; National Curriculum Programme of Study for Citizenship coverage 1b, 2a; links with QCA exemplar unit 4

Objective: To understand the law on racism and why it is important to take a stand against all forms of racism.

Resources

Copies of the school's bullying policy

Copies of Copymaster R11 'Developing relationships' (page 191)

Starter

Explain that the Race Relations Act of 1976 made racial discrimination unlawful. Read 'Racial discrimination and the law' (page 14) and explain the difference between direct discrimination and indirect discrimination. Talk about how the Race Relations Act of 2000 extended the law on indirect discrimination.

Suggested activities

● Read 'Racial attacks and harassment' (page 14). In pairs, students discuss what punishment they think offenders should receive for racial crimes. Should they be sent to prison, fined or made to pay compensation, or made to do community service? Does it depend on what their offence was? Discuss the view that in all cases of racial crimes the offender should be made to write an apology and/or to meet the victims and to apologise in person. Encourage them to share their views in a class discussion.

● Read 'Take a stand against racism' (page 15). In groups, discuss the advice it gives. Then read and discuss the four statements in 'What should I do?' (page 15). Share views in a class discussion.

● Ask groups to imagine they are part of a working group that has been asked to make proposals to improve race relations in the local community and to suggest measures to eradicate racism in their area. For example, what can the local police do? What can community workers do? What can local schools do? If the students had a budget of £50,000 to spend, how would they spend it? Ask the groups to draft a proposal to discuss with the rest of the class.

Plenary

Look at the school's bullying policy. Are there any special rules about racist bullying? Discuss how effective the students think the bullying policy is in dealing with racial bullying and any ways in which they think it could be improved.

Extension activities

Ask students to find out more information about how to beat racism by visiting websites such as www.childline.org.uk and www.kidscape.org.uk.

Encourage students to write a letter to a newspaper giving their views on racism and explaining why they think it important to take a stand against racism.

Recording and evaluating

Ask students to fill in the appropriate section of Copymaster R11 to record and evaluate what they learned from this unit.

UNIT 3 You and your decisions – how to make decisions

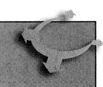

Your Life 3/Year 9

Lesson 1 *Your Life 3*, pages 16–17
National Framework for PSHE coverage 1a, 3i, 3j

Objective: To consider how good you are at making your own decisions, which people influence you and why.

Starter

Introduce the topic by asking: "Do you consider yourself to be good at making decisions or poor at making decisions?" "Do you make up your own mind or do you rely on what other people think?" Ask individuals to discuss with a partner how good they think they are at making decisions and to say why, giving examples that will support their opinion.

Suggested activities

- Ask students to do the quiz on page 16 ('Do you make your own decisions?'). Then invite them to talk with a partner about their quiz result, and to compare what it says about their decision-making ability with their own assessment.

- Ask individuals to study the list of important things to consider when making decisions (see 'In groups', page 16) and to rank them in order of importance, before sharing their views in a group and/or class discussion.

- Study the chart in 'Who influences you?' (page 17) and ask individuals to write down in order of importance five people who influence them. Then suggest they look at the list of reasons ('That person influences me because she/he …' page 17) and to write down why each person influences them. Then ask them to discuss in groups who influences them and why.

Plenary

Encourage the students to discuss what they have learned about who influences them and their decisions. Explain that they have been thinking about how people they come into contact with personally influence them, but that there are other influences too, most notably the media. How much do they think they are influenced by the media – by the views expressed in newspapers and magazines, in TV programmes, in songs, in books? What has the most influence on them – their family, their friends, the school, the local community, the media?

Extension activity

Ask students to reflect on a time when they had to make a difficult decision, by writing about it (see 'For your file', page 17).

Your Life 3/Year 9

UNIT 3 You and your decisions – how to make decisions

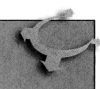

Your Life 3/Year 9

Lesson 2 *Your Life 3*, pages 18–19
National Framework for PSHE coverage 1a, 3i, 3j

Objective: To explore ways of making decisions, to understand what peer pressure is and to discuss ways of dealing with it.

Resources

Copies of Copymaster 3 'Consequences' (*Your Life 3 Copymasters*, page 15)

Copies of Copymaster R9 'Understanding yourself' (page 189)

Starter

Explain that all decisions have consequences. For example, if someone tells a lie, the consequence is that they lose someone else's trust if they are found out. Ask the students, in pairs, to list other examples of decisions they might take and the consequences that might follow, e.g. someone starts to smoke, truants, copies someone else's homework, shoplifts, goes joyriding, stays out all night. Then share some of the lists in a class discussion.

Suggested activities

- Read 'Consider the consequences' (page 18). Discuss with the class what it says about how we discover what is right and wrong, and the questions we need to ask ourselves when making decisions.

- Suggest groups discuss the statements in 'Right and wrong' (page 18) and to share their ideas in a class discussion.

- Read 'Stay in control of your life' (page 19). Discuss with the class what peer pressure is and the ways in which people will try to exert it. Do they agree with what the writer says about people who sink to such tactics? Talk about the difficulty of staying in control and saying "No" when friends are putting pressure on, and encourage them to practise saying "No" by doing the role-play activity (see page 19). Ask them to rate how well a person resists the pressure on a scale of 1 to 5 (1 = very well 5 = very badly).

Plenary

Read 'What to do when making decisions' (page 19). Discuss the five-point plan and suggest the students note down the mnemonic FACTS to help them to remember the plan.

Extension activities

Give out Copymaster 3 and ask groups to show their understanding of the consequences of different courses of action by discussing the situations, then sharing their views in a class discussion.

Ask students to develop role plays based on the three situations, or on other situations they can think of which involve difficult decisions, e.g. if they saw a friend cheating in an exam and then found out that the friend came top.

Recording and evaluating

Ask students to fill in the appropriate section of Copymaster R9 to record and evaluate what they learned from this unit.

UNIT 4 You and your family – becoming an adult

Your Life 3/Year 9

Lesson 1 *Your Life 3*, pages 20–21
National Framework for PSHE coverage 3e, 3g, 3h, 3i, 3k

> **Objective:** To explore the causes of tension between parents and teenagers, and to discuss ways of dealing with these difficulties.

Resources

Copies of Copymaster 4 'Parent problems' (*Your Life 3 Copymasters*, page 16)

Starter

Ask the students, in pairs, to brainstorm the things that cause tension and conflict between parents and teenagers, then make a class list on the board. Compare the class list with the 'Top ten causes of tension between parents and teenagers' on page 20. Hold a vote to decide which are the three main causes of tension.

Suggested activities

- Read 'How to deal with differences' (page 20). In pairs or groups, students draft details of other ground rules that Dave and his parents might have drawn up. Ask the students to use a word processor to produce a contract that parents and teenagers could agree upon. Suggest they compare their contracts in a class discussion.

- Ask groups to read and discuss the three viewpoints in the section 'How to get on better' (page 20). Prompt them to note down their views on a) how much independence they think parents should give teenagers, b) what teenagers can do to win parents' trust and c) how to improve communication between parents and teenagers. Ask them to share their views with the rest of the class.

- Read 'Arguments and how to survive them' and 'Educate your parents' (page 21). On their own, invite students to pick out what they consider to be the three most useful pieces of advice, then to share their views in a group and/or class discussion.

Plenary

Summarise the main pieces of advice about how to deal with arguments by teaching them the mnemonic BACKDOWN – Behave like an adult/Agree to listen/Consider what they say/Keep to the point/Don't lose your temper/Offer an apology if appropriate/Work to win their trust/Negotiate a compromise. Put a copy of the mnemonic on the wall for reference.

Extension activities

Act out the role play (see page 21). Ask some students to perform their role play to the rest of the class, and discuss how the different reactions of the teenager either escalated or defused the situation. Then ask students to do the writing activity (see 'For your file', page 21).

Read Copymaster 4 and ask groups to discuss the situations and the advice, then to report their views in a class discussion.

Ask students to role play and then make a tape recording of a radio phone-in programme in which an agony aunt or uncle offers advice to teenagers on how to deal with problems with parents.

Your Life 3/Year 9

UNIT 4 You and your family – becoming an adult

Your Life 3/Year 9

Lesson 2 *Your Life 3*, pages 22–23
National Framework for PSHE coverage 3e, 3g, 3h, 3i

Objective: To understand that in relationships a person has both rights and responsibilities, and to explore examples of taking responsibility within the family.

Resources

Copies of Copymaster R11 'Developing relationships' (page 191)

Starter

Read the introductory paragraph and 'My Bill of Rights' (page 22). Invite pairs to discuss the list of rights, ranking them in order of importance and adding any others rights they think are important. Then share their views with the rest of the class and discuss the responsibilities that they have to respect other people's rights.

Suggested activities

- Hold a class discussion of what causes tension between them and their brothers and sisters. Make a list on the board and compare the list with the top ten list on page 22. Then discuss the two statements (see 'In groups', page 22) about whether it is better to deal with problems with siblings yourself or through parents. Talk about how the advice they were discussing on how to deal with arguments with parents in the previous lesson applies to arguments with brothers and sisters. Remind them of the mnemonic 'BACKDOWN'.

- Read 'Taking responsibility' (page 23). Ask groups to discuss how the three people in the article took responsibility within their families, and to share experiences of times when they have taken responsibility for something within the family, e.g. for shopping when a parent was ill.

- Ask the students: "How responsible are you for things in your daily life at home? Do you get your own breakfast, do your own washing or feed your own pets?" Invite them to write a statement saying whether they think they take most of the responsibility, some of the responsibility or a little responsibility for things in their daily lives at home. Then read 'Who's responsible?' (page 23) and ask them, in pairs, to discuss whether they agree or disagree with Derek Stuart's views. Ask them to look at each other's statements and suggest ways that each of them might take more responsibility in their daily lives.

Plenary

Discuss the view that the more responsibility you take for your daily lives, the more your parents are likely to let you lead an independent life and make your own decisions. Invite them to say why they agree or disagree with this view.

Extension activity

Write an article for a teenage magazine about what causes arguments between brothers and sisters and how to deal with them. Give it a title, e.g. 'How to get on with your brothers and sisters'.

Recording and evaluating

Ask students to fill in the appropriate section of Copymaster R11 to record and evaluate what they learned from this unit.

UNIT 5 You and your values – human rights issues

Your Life 3/Year 9

Lesson 1 *Your Life 3*, pages 24–25
National Curriculum Programme of Study for Citizenship coverage 1a, 1i, 2a, 2b, 2c, 3a; links with QCA exemplar unit 3

Objective: To understand what basic human rights are and to illustrate how they are frequently violated.

Resources

Copies of Copymaster 5 'Rights and responsibilities' (*Your Life 3 Copymasters*, page 17)

Starter

Ask the students: "What are the basic rights that every human being has?" Hold a class discussion, listing the human rights they suggest on the board, before asking them to copy the list. Explain that with every right there comes the responsibility to respect other people's rights.

Suggested activities

● Ask the students, in pairs, to study the class list of human rights and to draw up a charter listing their top ten human rights. Invite them to share their views in a class discussion.

● Read 'Beyond the basics' (page 24). Talk about how and why the Universal Declaration of Human Rights was drawn up. Explain that it is not legally binding on UN member states and that, in order to provide a legal basis for human rights, the European Convention of Human Rights was passed and is now part of the UK legal system.

● Write the term 'violation' on the board and explain its meaning (an act which breaks, disregards or infringes a law, agreement or right). Read 'Violations of human rights' (page 24) and 'Case Study – Archana Guha' (page 25). Ask groups to discuss the various ways in which Archana Guha's rights were violated by the treatment she received and the way her case was handled after her release.

● Read 'Can torture ever be justified?' (page 25) and organise either a class discussion or a debate on the subject of torture.

Plenary

Hold a class discussion on how far it is our moral duty to protect the rights of people whose human rights are being violated. Discuss how we should treat dictators who are violating the human rights of the people in their country. Ask: "Is putting pressure on them by refusing to trade with them as far as we should go, or should we be prepared to go to war with them to remove them?" "Do we have the right to intervene and affect how another country is governed?"

Extension activities

Test the students understanding of rights and responsibilities by asking them to study Copymaster 5, to decide which are rights and which are responsibilities, then to compare their answers with a partner and to list further examples of rights and responsibilities.

Ask students to find up-to-date information on current human rights issues by visiting internet websites such as www.humanrights.britishcouncil.org.

Your Life 3/Year 9

UNIT 5 You and your values – human rights issues

Lesson 2 *Your Life 3*, pages 26–27
National Curriculum Programme of Study for Citizenship coverage 1a, 1f, 1i, 2a, 2b, 2c, 3a; links with QCA exemplar unit 3

Objective: To explore issues connected with the right to freedom of thought and the right to freedom of expression, and to explain the work of Amnesty International.

Resources

Video clip of a satirical TV programme, e.g. Rory Bremner

Starter

Explain that in the UK we live in a free society – that is, we are free to exercise our rights to practise whatever religion we like, and to say what we like, i.e. we have free speech and a free media. This means we can openly criticise and even make fun of the government. Explain what satire is (something, such as a programme or piece of writing, that ridicules the behaviour of people or events). Either show a video clip of a satirical programme or talk about satirical comedians who appear on TV, and satirical programmes such as *Have I Got News For You* and satirical magazines such as *Private Eye*. Explain that the right to freedom of thought and freedom of expression are two key articles in the Universal Declaration of Human Rights.

Suggested activities

- Read Article 18 of the Universal Declaration of Human Rights and Ngawang's story ('Freedom of thought', page 26). Ask groups to discuss the two views of what Ngawang did. Explain what a martyr is. In a class discussion, talk about people who have been prepared to die rather than give up their religious beliefs. Ask: "How far would you be prepared to go if your rights were being denied you?" "Are there any circumstances in which using force to obtain your rights can be justified?"

- Read 'Conscientious objectors' (page 26). Then invite individuals to study the three statements and to write a short statement expressing their views about pacifists. Encourage them to share their views in a group discussion.

- Read 'Jailed for joking' (page 27), then, in groups, discuss what 'freedom of expression' means and whether there should be any censorship of the internet. Ask: "How could censorship of the internet work?" "Who would decide what is to be allowed and not allowed?"

- Explain what Amnesty International is. Read and discuss 'Amnesty International' (page 27).

Plenary

Ask groups to prepare a short statement saying how important they think freedom of expression is. Invite them to share their statements with the rest of the class.

Extension activity

Ask students to collect examples of human rights violations around the world from newspapers and the internet. Display them in the classroom.

UNIT 5 You and your values – human rights issues

Lesson 3 *Your Life 3*, pages 28–29
National Framework for PSHE coverage 3a; National Curriculum Programme of Study for Citizenship coverage 1a, 1i, 2a, 2b, 2c, 3a; links with QCA exemplar unit 3

Objective: To explore women's rights and equal opportunities issues in the UK and around the world.

Resources

Copies of the school's equal opportunities policy

Copies of Copymaster 17A 'Understanding human rights' (page 173)

Copies of Copymaster R12 'Developing as a citizen' (page 192)

Starter

Hold a class discussion on equal opportunities at school. Ask: "Does your school treat girls and boys equally?" Look at the school's equal opportunities policy. How effective is it in stopping discrimination? For example, do the school uniform rules discriminate against girls? Are the lessons 'gender inclusive', i.e. do teachers stress women's achievements as much as men's? Invite groups to rate how girl-friendly the school is on a scale of 1–10 (1 = very low, 10 = very high). Share their views.

Suggested activities

- Read 'Women's rights in the UK' and 'Discrimination at work' (page 28). In pairs, ask students to discuss why they think women's pay still lags behind men's and why men still dominate the highest-paid jobs. Then hold a group discussion. Read 'The right to fight' (page 28). Hold a class discussion answering these questions: Should some jobs should be restricted to either males or females only?

- In pairs, study 'Iran's female students protest at segregation' (page 29). Discuss what a newspaper editorial supporting the students' action would say. Then discuss what an editorial condemning their actions would say. Read 'Violence against women' (page 29). Then, in groups, discuss the two questions about violence and sexual harassment (see 'In groups', page 29).

Plenary

Ask students to discuss what sort of behaviour they think are examples of sexual harassment. Talk about what action they think should be taken against anyone who sexually harasses someone either at work, in public or at school.

Extension activity

Ask groups to either draft a letter to the minister for women saying what they think her priorities should be or a proposal to the school council saying what they think needs to be done to improve equal opportunities at the school.

Assessment

Use copies of Copymaster 17A to assess the students' understanding of human rights. Answers: 1. home, 2. Universal, 3. Amnesty, 4. Strasbourg, 5. violence, 6. Discrimination, 7. trial, 8. thought, 9. child, 10. torture, 11. conscientious.

Recording and evaluating

Ask students to use the appropriate section of Copymaster R12 to record and evaluate what they have learned from this unit.

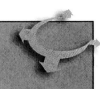

UNIT 6 You and your feelings – dealing with loss

Your Life 3/Year 9

Lesson 1 *Your Life 3*, pages 30–32
National Framework for PSHE coverage 1d, 3e

> **Objective:** To explore how you may feel when someone close to you dies, to discuss how to cope with those feelings and how you can help someone who has been bereaved.

Resources

Copies of Copymaster 6 'Helping someone who has been bereaved' (*Your Life 3 Copymasters*, page 18)

Starter

Explain that when someone close to you dies there is always a feeling of shock – especially if it's sudden and unexpected. You're bound to be sad too. Write 'shock' and 'sadness' on the board and explain that you may also feel other emotions. Write 'AARG!' on the board and explain that it stands for Anger Anxiety Resentment and Guilt. Explain that these are other feelings you may experience when grieving after a death.

Suggested activities

- Read 'How you may feel after a death' (page 30). Discuss with the class what they learn from this article about the different feelings that people who are bereaved may experience and why they have them.

- Read 'Showing emotions' (page 31). In groups, discuss what the writer says about expressing grief, about how long grief lasts and why she suggests that talking helps. Ask individuals to draw up a list of 'Dos' and 'Don'ts' about how to cope with grief, then invite them to share their ideas in a class discussion.

- Read 'Funerals' (page 31). Ask pairs to discuss the arguments for and against children (whatever age they are) attending the funeral of a close relative or friend. Then share your views in a class discussion.

- Ask individuals to do the quiz 'Can you help a friend in need?' (page 32), then to join up with a partner to compare their answers and to read the answers together.

Plenary

Ask the students to write down what they think were the most important things they learned from this lesson about grief, how to cope with it and how to help someone who is experiencing it. Then encourage some students to read their ideas to the class.

Extension activities

Ask groups to read Copymaster 6 and to discuss the advice it gives on what to do when someone they know has been bereaved. Then ask them to draft a letter to Gera who has asked for advice on what to do because she has a friend, Howard, whose teenage sister has died in a road accident.

Ask students to investigate what the charities Cruse (www.crusebereavementcare.org.uk) and Winston's Wish (www.winstonswish.org.uk) do to help people who have been bereaved.

UNIT 6 You and your feelings – dealing with loss

Lesson 2 *Your Life 3*, page 33
National Framework for PSHE coverage 3c, 3e

Objective: To examine the feelings you may experience when a close relationship ends and to explore how to cope with rejection.

Resources

Copies of Copymaster R9 'Understanding yourself' (page 189)

Starter

Write the word 'recrimination' on the board and explain that it means making accusations about someone's behaviour. Talk about how, when a relationship comes to an end, we may feel rejection and that the feelings we experience may be similar to those of the grief we feel when a person close to us dies. Explain that we may be tempted to indulge in recriminations, either self-recrimination or accusing a former friend of doing things that caused you to drift apart, but that recrimination is not productive.

Suggested activities

- Read the article by Erica Stewart on page 33. Ask groups to discuss the advice she gives, then to make a list of 'Dos' and 'Don'ts' on how to cope with rejection and to share their views in a class discussion.

- Ask students to read the advice Louisa Fairbanks gives about how to end a relationship in 'Announcing it's over' (page 33), to discuss in groups whether they agree with it and to decide on the best way to end a relationship.

- Invite the students to write letters in reply to a penfriend on how to cope with the ending of a relationship (see 'For your file', page 33).

Plenary

Ask some of the students to read out their letters. Discuss which of their letters gives the best advice and why.

Extension activity

Ask students to imagine they work for a teenage magazine. Their task is to write an article entitled 'Pat's story' in which they tell the story of how a teenager coped with the break-up of a relationship which had lasted for 18 months.

Recording and evaluating

Invite students to use the appropriate section of Copymaster R9 to record and evaluate what they learned from this unit.

UNIT 7 You and your body – drugs and drugtaking

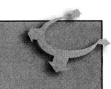

Your Life 3/Year 9

Lesson 1 *Your Life 3*, pages 34–35
National Framework for PSHE coverage 2d

> **Objective:** To explore the factors which affect the risk involved in drugtaking and to provide information about solvent abuse.

Starter

Introduce the topic by explaining that while all drugtaking involves risks, the risks involved vary. Ask the students on their own to write down what they consider to be the risks of a) taking ecstasy, b) smoking cannabis and c) injecting heroin. Hold a class discussion in which they share some of their ideas. Explain that how dangerous drugtaking is depends on the drug that is taken, the person taking it and how and where it is taken.

Suggested activities

- Ask individuals to read the article 'How dangerous is drugtaking?' (page 34) and to make notes under the headings: 'The drug and its effects', 'The person', 'The environment'. Then invite groups to discuss the main points they have learned from the article about the factors that influence how dangerous drugtaking is.

- Ask individuals to write an article explaining 'Why drugtaking is a risky business' (see 'For your file', page 34).

- Ask pairs to study the article 'Solvent abuse' (page 35), then to produce a list of key facts about solvent abuse, entitled 'Ten things you should know about solvent abuse'.

Plenary

Ask the students to imagine they are designing a poster to make young people aware of the risks involved in taking drugs, and to decide what main points they would try to put across.

Extension activity

Invite groups to draw up plans for a two-minute public information video designed to warn young people of the risks of drugtaking. Ask someone from each group to present their ideas to the rest of the class for the class to rate how good the proposal is on a five-point scale (1 = excellent to 5 = poor).

Your Life 3/Year 9

UNIT 7 You and your body – drugs and drugtaking

Your Life 3/Year 9

Lesson 2 *Your Life 3*, pages 36–37
National Framework for PSHE coverage 2d, 2h

> **Objective:** To examine the problems drugs can cause, to explain how to help a friend with a drug problem and what to do in an emergency caused by drugtaking.

Resources

Copies of Copymaster 7 'Drugs problems' (*Your Life 3 Copymasters*, page 19)

Copies of Copymaster R10 'Keeping healthy' (page 190)

Starter

Ask: "What problems can a person have if they take drugs?" Invite pairs to brainstorm their ideas and then share them in a brief class discussion. Point out that: health problems can be mental as well as physical; drugtaking can affect relationships with family and friends; it can cause a person to steal in order to pay for drugs; it can affect their work.

Suggested activities

- Read 'My life's a mess' (page 36), then invite the class to discuss how drugtaking has affected Sarah's life. Then read 'How to help a friend who has a problem with drugs' (page 36). Prompt pairs to imagine they are Sarah's friends, to decide what they would say to try to help her and to role play a scene in which they talk to Sarah.

- Ask individuals to write Melanie's reply to Shania, offering advice on how she can help a friend with a drugs problem (see 'For your file', page 36).

- Read 'What to do in an emergency' (page 37). Ask pairs to draw up a ten-question test based on the information given in the article, e.g. 'Question 1: Name two drugs which may cause someone to become tense and panicky'. Then ask them to join up with another pair, to swap tests and to answer each other's questions. Ask individuals to write an imaginary account of giving emergency first aid to someone who becomes ill after taking drugs (see 'For your file', page 37).

Plenary

Recap how to give emergency first aid, focusing on overheating and dehydration. Remind them of steps to prevent it occurring, what the warning signs are and what to do if someone overheats.

Extension activities

Study the letters about drugs problems on Copymaster 7 and ask groups to discuss the advice that the drugs counsellor gives. Ask them to decide which they think are the most useful pieces of advice and why, and hold a class discussion.

Ask students to use the internet to research information and advice on drugs problems. Useful websites include www.mindbodysoul.gov.uk.

Invite a member of the local St John Ambulance branch to talk about how to give emergency first aid to someone who has become ill after taking drugs.

Recording and evaluating

Ask the students to fill in the appropriate section of Copymaster R10 to record and evaluate what they learned from this unit.

Your Life 3/Year 9

UNIT 8 You and the law – crimes and punishments

Lesson 1 *Your Life 3*, pages 38–39
National Curriculum Programme of Study for Citizenship coverage 1a, 2a, 2b, 2c; links with QCA exemplar units 2, 15

Objective: To explore why so many young people commit crimes and to discuss shoplifting.

Starter

Explain that young people commit one in three crimes of burglary, theft and criminal damage. Ask: "Why do so many young people get involved in crime?" Write students' suggestions on the board, e.g. to show off, to rebel, to take revenge on society because they're unhappy, to get a thrill, to get money for things they can't afford, because they get drunk or high, to be 'one of the gang'.

Suggested activities

● Read 'Why do so many young people commit crimes?' (page 38). Invite groups to discuss the reasons given in the article and to compare them with their own suggestions. What do they think are the main reasons?

● Read 'More girls turn to crime' (page 38). Ask pairs to discuss the reasons given in the article, to suggest any other reasons and to share their views in a class discussion.

● Study the information on shoplifting and 'Rebecca's story' (page 39). Ask students to write answers to the four questions (see 'In groups', page 39) and then to share their views in a group and/or class discussion.

● Ask individuals to write a story about a young person who is caught shoplifting ('For your file', page 39).

Plenary

End with a general discussion on stealing. What are the students' attitudes to different forms of stealing, e.g. fare dodging, fraud, robbery, burglary, shoplifting? Are some forms of stealing more serious than others or are all forms of stealing equally wrong? Should anyone caught stealing always be taken to the police?

Extension activity

Develop a role play of a TV studio discussion on the issues raised in the lesson by suggesting that some of the students act as a panel of people with differing views on why there is so much youth crime. The other members of the class can act as the studio audience, and the person chairing the discussion can invite them to give their views.

Your Life 3/Year 9

UNIT 8 You and the law – crimes and punishments

Your Life 3/Year 9

Lesson 2 *Your Life 3*, pages 40–41
National Curriculum Programme of Study for Citizenship coverage 1a, 2a, 2b, 2c; links with QCA exemplar units 2, 15

> **Objective:** To explore the aims of punishment, to discuss the effectiveness of imprisonment and to consider what different types of punishment should be given for particular crimes.

Resources

Copies of Copymaster 8 'A punishment to fit the crime' (*Your Life 3 Copymasters*, page 20)

Starter

Ask the students: "What should the aims of punishment be?" and list their ideas on the board. Explain that there are five main theories about punishment. Write the words 'deterrence', 'protection', 'reform', 'retribution' and 'reparation' on the board, explain their meanings and ask the students to study the chart at the top of page 40.

Suggested activities

- Read 'Imprisonment – does it work?' and 'A country without prisons' (page 40). Then invite groups to discuss the four statements about prisons, to decide whether they agree with them and to share their views in a class discussion.

- Talk about the different types of punishment that can be given and read 'A dictionary of punishments' (page 41). Ask individuals to write down what punishments they would give the seven people a) if they were first-time offenders and b) if they were repeat offenders (see 'In groups', page 41), then to share their views in a group discussion.

- Read 'What about the victim?' (page 41). Ask groups to discuss how far the effect on the victim should be taken into consideration when deciding a punishment, then to share their views in a class discussion.

Plenary

Discuss all the things that magistrates need to take into account when deciding what punishment to give someone, e.g. the type of crime, the severity of the crime, how much the victim has suffered, the age of the offender, whether or not they have offended before, the purpose of the punishment, the effect it is likely to have on the offender. Ask: "What should the magistrate's main consideration be?"

Extension activities

Ask groups to do the activity on Copymaster 8 (to draw up lists of crimes in categories according to how serious they consider them to be and to decide on maximum and minimum punishments for each offence).

Ask pairs to discuss their views on prisons (see 'In pairs' on Copymaster 8), then each to write their views on how prison should be used as a punishment.

Invite individuals to use the internet to research information about prisons and alternatives to prisons, e.g. by visiting websites such as www.nacro.org (the website of the National Association for the Care and Resettlement of Offenders).

Your Life 3/Year 9

UNIT 8 You and the law – crimes and punishments

Your Life 3/Year 9

Lesson 3 *Your Life 3*, pages 42–43
National Curriculum Programme of Study for Citizenship coverage 1a, 2a, 2b, 2c; links with QCA exemplar units 2, 15

Objective: To examine ways of treating young offenders in order to reduce crime and to explain what youth action groups are.

Resources

Copies of Copymaster 18A 'Understanding crimes and punishment' (page 174)

Copies of Copymaster R12 'Developing as a citizen' (page 192)

Starter

Ask: "What's the best way to treat young offenders in order to reduce crime?" Invite the students to imagine that a Home Office minister has asked them to suggest one action that the government should take, which would reduce the amount of youth crime. Ask them to brainstorm their ideas in groups, then hold a class discussion.

Suggested activities

- Read 'How can crime be reduced?' (page 42). Ask groups to discuss the four ways of dealing with young offenders, then discuss with the class their views on what is most likely to reduce crime. Ask individuals to write a short statement expressing their views on what measures they think would be the most effective in cutting down youth crime. **AO**

- Read the two articles on 'Youth Action Groups' (page 43). In groups, then as a class, ask the students to discuss ideas for Youth Action Group projects and for setting up a Youth Action Group in their area. Draft a proposal for the class representative to put to the school council.

- Read 'Don't ignore crime – take action!' (page 43). Suggest groups discuss the arguments for and against 'having a go', decide on the circumstances in which a person should intervene, then share their views in a class discussion.

Plenary

Ask some students to read out their statements and to recap the measures they think would be most effective in helping to reduce youth crime.

Extension activities

Students research other Youth Action Group projects, visiting The Home Office Crime Prevention website (www.homeoffice.gov.uk/crimeprev).

Assessment

Use copies of Copymaster 18A to assess the students' understanding of crimes and punishments.

Recording and evaluating

Ask the students to use the appropriate section of Copymaster R12 to record and evaluate what they learned from this unit.

UNIT 9 You and other people – being assertive

Your Life 3/Year 9

Lesson 1 *Your Life 3*, pages 44–45
National Framework for PSHE coverage 1b, 1c, 3a, 3i, 3k

> **Objective:** To understand the difference between assertive, aggressive and passive behaviour.

Resources

Copies of Copymaster 9 'How assertive are you?' (*Your Life 3 Copymasters*, page 21).

Starter

Write the words 'assertive', 'aggressive' and 'passive' on the board. Explain that these describe, in broad terms, how people behave in their dealings with other people. Give an example: "Your sister has an irritating habit which is getting on your nerves." Explain that getting angry and shouting at her about it would be aggressive, saying nothing would be passive, but talking to her calmly about it and why it irritates you would be assertive. Then read the introductory text on page 44.

Suggested activities

- Ask the students, in pairs, to study the chart at the top of page 45. They then discuss the ten situations and write down what would be assertive, aggressive and passive behaviour in each situation. Ask them to compare their answers with other pairs in a group discussion. Then, as a class, discuss why in each case the best way to handle the situation is to be assertive.

- Invite pairs to choose one of the situations and to role play it in three different ways. Alternatively, ask them to write contrasting scripts showing a person behaving assertively in one script and either passively or aggressively in another.

- Read 'It doesn't pay to be passive' (page 44). Discuss, as a class, what the article says about why people sometimes behave passively, and what the consequences of behaving passively are.

Plenary

Without referring to the chart on page 44, ask pairs to make a list of the various ways an assertive person behaves. Check their lists against the chart and discuss with them why it is preferable for someone to behave assertively rather than aggressively or passively.

Extension activity

Give out copies of Copymaster 9 and ask students to complete the quiz individually. Then discuss, in pairs, what they learned about how assertive they are.

UNIT 9 You and other people – being assertive

Your Life 3/Year 9

Lesson 2 *Your Life 3*, pages 46–47
National Framework for PSHE coverage 1b, 1c, 3a, 3i, 3k

Objective: To understand assertiveness techniques and how to use them.

Resources

Copies of Copymaster R11 'Developing relationships' (page 191).

Starter

Remind the students of the differences between assertive, aggressive and passive behaviour explained in Lesson 1, of the consequences of behaving aggressively or passively, and of the benefits of behaving assertively.

Suggested activities

- Read the article 'How to be assertive' (page 46). Ask individuals to take notes on the key points, then, as a class, discuss the advice it gives.

- Invite pairs to study the list 'Assertiveness dos and don'ts' (page 46) and to discuss the reasons for each piece of advice.

- Read 'Saying what you want – confidence tips' (page 47). Ask groups to discuss each of the six steps and to decide which two pieces of advice are the most useful. Then share their views in a class discussion.

- Ask pairs to practise being assertive by performing the role plays (page 47). Alternatively, if the lesson is taking place in a classroom where it is impossible to do role plays, invite pairs to script rather than to act out the scenes, then to take it in turns to read them aloud.

Plenary

Hold a class discussion. Ask: "Is it easier to talk about being assertive than to be assertive in practice?" "Is it harder to be assertive with your family and friends than it is to be assertive with people you don't know well?" "How important do you think it is to develop assertiveness skills?" "What are the key things you have learned from the lesson about how to be assertive?"

Extension activity

Ask individuals to write a story describing a situation – either real or imaginary – in which a person behaves assertively, and consequently brings about an important change in their life (by altering the situation, changing a relationship or developing their self-esteem).

Recording and evaluating

Invite students to fill in the appropriate section of Copymaster R11 to record and evaluate what they have learned from this unit.

UNIT 10 You and the media – the power of the press

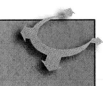

Your Life 3/Year 9

Lesson 1 *Your Life 3*, pages 48–49
National Curriculum Programme of Study for Citizenship coverage 1h, 2a, 2b, 2c; links with QCA exemplar unit 9

Objective: To examine the press in Britain, exploring the issues of press ownership, news management and what controls the content of newspapers.

Resources

Copies of two or three newspapers from the same day

Copies of Copymaster 10 'Telling it straight?' (*Your Life 3 Copymasters*, page 22)

Copies of Copymaster 19A 'Understanding the press' (page 175)

Starter

Explain what is meant by 'a free press' and how it is free from government controls. Discuss how in undemocratic states there is state control of the press through censorship. Point out that even in democracies there is some censorship of news that might threaten national security. Then read 'The power of the government' (page 48).

Suggested activities

- Read 'The power of the owners' and 'The power of the Sun' (page 48). Ask groups to discuss their views on newspaper ownership and proprietors controlling the political message their newspapers give, then to share their views in a class discussion.

- Explain what spin doctoring is. Talk about what a press release is and how big businesses and political parties time press releases so they appear to coincide with the issuing of reports. Then read and discuss with the class 'News management' (page 48).

- Read 'What controls the content of newspapers?' (page 49). Then invite groups to study copies of two or three different newspapers, to compare the different space given to different kinds of reports and to discuss what this tells us about the news values of the different newspapers.

- Read 'Public interest versus private rights' (page 49). As a class, discuss the issues it raises, focusing in particular on the two statements (see 'In groups', page 49).

Plenary

Sum up in a class discussion what the students have learned about the different influences on the content of newspapers in Britain.

Extension activity

Ask groups to study the article 'Telling it straight?' on Copymaster 10, to discuss the issues it raises, then to share their views in a class discussion.

Assessment

Use copies of Copymaster 19A to assess students' understanding of press issues.

UNIT 10 You and the media – the power of the press

Your Life 3/Year 9

Lesson 2 *Your Life 3*, pages 50–51
National Curriculum Programme of Study for Citizenship coverage 1h, 2a, 2b, 2c; links with QCA exemplar unit 9

Objective: To explore how young people are presented by the press and to discuss teenage magazines.

Resources

Copies of recent newspapers and copies of teenage magazines

Copies of Copymaster R12 'Developing as a citizen' (page 192)

Starter

Ask the students: "How are young people presented in the press? Are they largely ignored?" "Does the press focus enough on young people and their interests?" "Are young people patronised by the press?" Do you think the press stereotype young people?" Invite them to share their views in a class discussion.

Suggested activities

- Read 'Kids: what the papers say' (page 50). Ask groups to discuss what the article says about stereotyping young people, then allow them to share their views in a class discussion.

- Give out copies of recent newspapers. Ask pairs to look for articles about young people and to discuss the image of young people they give. They can cut out the articles, write comments on them and mount them to make a wall display.

- Ask individuals to write a letter to the editor of a newspaper, expressing their views on the way young people are presented by the press.

- Read 'What do you think of teenage magazines?' (page 51). Ask groups to discuss the views expressed in the article, then to share their own views in a class discussion.

- Ask groups to draft proposals for a new teenage magazine, and to present their ideas in a class discussion.

Plenary

Discuss how the students' ideas for new teenage magazines differ from existing magazines. How does their view of what teenagers want to read differ from adults' views?

Extension activities

Ask pairs or groups of students to carry out a detailed study of a teenage magazine (see 'For your file', page 51).

Prompt groups to imagine they have been asked to edit a page for young people to appear weekly in a national newspaper. Ask them to draw up proposals for its contents, and to discuss them with the rest of the class. They could then work together as a class to prepare articles, to design and produce a specimen page.

Recording and evaluating

Invite students to use the appropriate section of Copymaster R12 to help them to record and evaluate what they learned from this unit.

UNIT 11 You and your money – banking and ways of saving

> **Objective:** To understand what bank accounts are, and how to choose and open a bank account.

Starter

Introduce the topic of bank accounts by explaining that there are two main types – current accounts and savings accounts. Discuss how current accounts are designed for adults to use for their everyday needs and offer them a safe and easy way of handling their money. Explain how current account holders get a debit card to buy things and get cash from machines, and that they can use cheques or direct debits to pay bills. But you get only a small amount of interest on a current account. So savings accounts are more suitable for teenagers.

Suggested activities

- Read 'Banks – What do they offer?' and 'So you want to open a bank account? Your questions answered' (page 52). Suggest the students discuss, in groups, what the articles say about having a bank account and how to open one, then, as a class, prompt them to discuss whether or nor they think it's a good idea to have a bank account.

- Ask pairs to role play a scene in which one person explains to a friend why they think it's worth having a bank account. Then, individually, ask them to write a letter explaining the advantages of having a bank account and how to open one (see 'For your file', page 52).

- Read 'Which bank is best for you?' (page 53). Ask groups to discuss which bank account they would choose and why, then to explain their choice in a class discussion.

Plenary

Recap the advantages of having a bank account and how to go about opening it.

Extension activities

Encourage groups to conduct a survey of bank accounts which are currently available to young people in your area, either by visiting local branches or telephoning them to obtain information. Then ask them to report their findings in a class discussion, saying which of the accounts they would recommend and why.

Organise a visit from a local bank manager to talk about bank accounts for young people. Ask the students to prepare for the visit by drawing up a list of questions.

Your Life 3/Year 9

UNIT 11 You and your money – banking and ways of saving

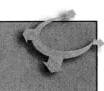

Your Life 3/Year 9

Lesson 2 *Your Life 3*, pages 54–55
National Framework for PSHE coverage 1g

Objective: To understand and to compare different forms of saving.

Resources

Copies of Copymaster 11 'An A–Z of financial terms' (*Your Life 3 Copymasters*, page 23)

Copies of Copymaster R9 'Understanding yourself' (page 189)

Starter

Discuss how, if you want to save money, you need to ask a number of questions, e.g. How safe is my money? How accessible is my money? Is there a guarantee that I will earn a certain amount of interest? Will I have to pay tax on the money I invest? Make a list on the board of all the questions students need to think about when deciding where to put their savings.

Suggested activities

- Read the explanations of the various ways of saving on pages 54 and 55, and answer any questions students have about each method. Then ask groups to list the advantages and disadvantages of each type of saving and to decide which they would recommend to a young person and which they would recommend to an adult. Ask: "Would it make a difference according to how much money the person was saving?"

- Invite pairs to discuss whether they would put £100 into national savings certificates or premium bonds (see 'In pairs', page 55).

- Give out copies of Copymaster 11 and test students' understanding by challenging pairs to compile a glossary of financial terms for their files. **AO**

Plenary

Recap the information given on these pages by giving the class a quick quiz consisting of true and false statements, e.g. 'You get interest on the money you invest in premium bonds'; 'The interest you earn from ISAs is tax-free'.

Extension activity

Ask pairs of students to pick a company that is listed on the stock market and to follow the progress of its shares over a month by looking at the share values in a daily newspaper or on the internet. Then ask them to report how much their money would have increased or decreased in value if they had bought £1000 worth of shares in that company at the beginning of the month. You could explain what the FTSE 100 is and allow them to compare the movement in their shares' values with the movement of the FTSE 100.

Recording and evaluating

Ask students to fill in the appropriate section of Copymaster R9 to record and evaluate what they learned from this unit.

UNIT 12 You and your body – eating disorders

Your Life 3/Year 9

Lesson 1 *Your Life 3*, pages 56–57
National Framework for PSHE coverage 2b, 2f

Objective: To explain what anorexia nervosa is, to explore what triggers it and to discuss how it affects people

---

Resources

Copies of Copymaster 12 'The diet trap' (*Your Life 3 Copymasters*, page 24)

Starter

Remind the students that in order to stay healthy we need to eat a balanced diet (that is, the right amounts of the right foods). A balanced diet consisting of a range of foods gives us enough proteins for our bodies to grow, enough energy for our physical needs, enough vitamins to keep us healthy, and enough fibre to help us get rid of waste. Remind them that if we eat too much we may get obese, and if we eat too little we may become ill through lack of nutrition.

Suggested activities

- Read 'Anorexia nervosa' (page 56) and 'The red flags of an eating disorder' (page 57). Discuss, as a class, what the articles say about anorexia and what the signs of an eating disorder are.

- Read 'Portia's story' (page 56) and 'Mark's story' (page 57). Discuss, as a class, what they learn from them about what triggers anorexia and how anorexia affects people's lives.

- Study 'What causes an eating disorder?' (page 57) and discuss with the class what the factors are that may cause an eating disorder. Talk about how helping a person with anorexia involves trying to sort out the underlying cause of the illness, in addition to getting them to eat more.

Plenary

Sum up the key facts the students have learned in the lesson by holding a class discussion and listing on the board 'Ten things you should know about anorexia'.

Extension activity

Give out copies of Copymaster 12. Ask groups to study it and discuss what it says about why people diet, what are bad reasons for dieting, what is the only good reason and what dieting does to you in adolescence. Then invite them individually to write a letter to a friend who is planning to go on a diet, explaining why they don't think it's a good idea.

Your Life 3/Year 9

Your Life 3/Year 9

Lesson 2 *Your Life 3*, pages 58–59
National Framework for PSHE coverage 2b, 2f

Objective: To examine bulimia and to discuss media pressure on young people to be a particular size and shape.

Resources

Copies of Copymaster R10 'Keeping healthy' (page 190)

Starter

Recap on what the students learned about anorexia in the previous lesson. Explain that there are other eating disorders which involve eating too much rather than eating too little (compulsive overeating which causes obesity, and bulimia which involves binge-eating and purging).

Suggested activities

- Read 'What is bulimia?' and 'What to do if a friend has bulimia ...' (page 58). Invite individuals to make notes on what bulimics do, what causes bulimia and what to do if a friend has bulimia. Then allow them to discuss what they have learned about bulimia in groups.

- Read the two articles on page 59 ('Skinny models "send unhealthy message"' and 'Is there too much pressure to be thin?' Ask them, in groups, to discuss whether they agree with the views expressed by the three teenagers, then to share their views in a class discussion.

- Ask groups to discuss Adele Lovell's statement (see 'In groups', page 59), before writing their own statement about what they think matters most – personality or looks – and giving their views on the effects of media pressure. **AO**

Plenary

Conclude the lesson by allowing some of the students to read out their statements and discussing how far there is general agreement on the issues that have been raised about the importance of personality and looks, and the influence of media pressure.

Extension activities

Ask students to find out more about eating disorders using the internet. Useful websites to visit include Mirror Mirror (www.mirror-mirror.org/eatdis.htm) and the Eating Disorders Association (www.edauk.com).

Recording and evaluating

Ask students to fill in the appropriate section of Copymaster R10 to record and evaluate what they learned from this unit.

Your Life 3/Year 9

UNIT 13 You and the community – local government and local organisations

Your Life 3/Year 9

Lesson 1 *Your Life 3*, pages 60–61
National Curriculum Programme of Study for Citizenship coverage 1c, 2a, 3b, 3c; links with QCA exemplar unit 7

Objective: To understand how local government is organised, how it is financed and the services which local authorities provide.

Starter

Introduce the topic by drawing a diagram on the board to explain that there are three tiers of government in the United Kingdom: 1) central government, consisting of the two Houses of Parliament; 2) regional government – the Scottish Parliament, the Welsh Assembly, the Northern Ireland Assembly and the Greater London Assembly; 3) local government, consisting of local councils. Challenge the class to tell you as much as they can about your local council (its name, its responsibilities and how it is funded).

Suggested activities

● Read 'How local government is organised' (page 60) and 'How local government is financed' (page 60). Discuss, as a class, what they learn from the articles about the structure and funding of local government. Debate the arguments for and against replacing council tax with a local income tax.

● Read 'Local authority services' (page 61). Ask the students, in pairs, to design an A4-sized information leaflet with the aim of informing people 'What your local council does for you' or 'What your local councils do for you', depending on whether the system in your area is one-tier or two-tier.

● Invite groups to imagine they are local councillors faced with the need to save money on their budget, to discuss the ten ways of doing so and to choose three (see 'In groups', page 61). Then share their decisions in a class discussion.

Plenary

Ask the students to make notes on what they have learned about their local council (or councils), their responsibilities, how they are funded and how they differ from councils in areas which have a different system.

Extension activities

Ask pairs to research local government in your area by contacting the local council for information and by visiting the relevant local government pages on the Department of the Environment, Transport and the Regions website (www.detr.gov.uk).

UNIT 13 You and the community – local government and local organisations

Your Life 3/Year 9

Lesson 2 *Your Life 3*, pages 62–63
National Curriculum Programme of Study for Citizenship coverage 1c, 2a, 3b, 3c; links with QCA exemplar unit 7

> **Objective:** To explain how local councils are elected, who local councillors are and what they do, and to discuss the reasons why some areas have directly elected mayors and youth councils.

Resources

Copies of Copymaster 13 'How much do you know about local government?' (*Your Life 3 Copymasters*, page 25)

Local authority leaflets on the services the local authority provides (optional)

Copies of Copymaster 20A 'Understanding local government' (page 176)

Copies of Copymaster R12 'Developing as a citizen' (page 192)

Starter

Remind the students of all the services that are provided by local councils and make a list on the board (see 'Local authority services', page 61). Show them any leaflets that your local council produces about the services it provides. Explain that while people are quick to complain when a local authority service lets them down or their council tax goes up, the turnout at local elections is very low.

Suggested activities

- Read 'Local elections' (page 62). Discuss how councils are elected and what your local electoral system is. Discuss whether students think not voting in local elections is due to the complexity of the system or apathy. Would changes to the voting system change the level of the turnout? (See 'In groups', page 62.)

- Read 'Bill paves way for directly elected mayors' (page 62). In groups or as a class discuss the idea of having directly-elected mayors. Ask groups to read and discuss 'What do councillors do?' and 'Who can be a councillor?' (page 63), before sharing their views on why they would or would not ever volunteer to be a councillor.

- Read 'Giving teenagers a voice' (page 63). In groups, ask students to share their ideas on youth councils, before writing a letter expressing their views.

Plenary

Write on the board: 'The local council is important to everyone and everyone should vote in local elections because …'. How would students finish this?

Extension activities

Test students' understanding of local government by getting them to answer the questions on Copymaster 13. Answers: 1. true, 2. false, 3. true, 4. false, 5. false, 6. false, 7. true, 8. true, 9. false, 10. true, 11. false, 12. true.

Assessment

AO

Use Copymaster 20A to assess understanding of local government.

Recording and evaluating

Ask students to use the appropriate section of Copymaster R12 to help them to record and evaluate what they learned from this unit.

UNIT 14 You and your opinions – which political party do you support?

Your Life 3/Year 9

Lesson 1 *Your Life 3*, pages 64–66
National Curriculum Programme of Study for Citizenship coverage 1d, 1e, 1f, 2a, 2b, 2c, 3b; links with QCA exemplar units 6, 12

Objective: To explain what political parties are, which political parties there are in the UK and what they stand for.

Resources

Copies of Copymaster 21A 'Understanding political parties and their policies' (page 177)

Starter

Explain what a political party is (a group of people who share common ideas about how a country should be governed). Introduce the terms 'left-wing' and 'right-wing' and explain how, in broad terms, left-wing parties are radical parties which favour change, while right-wing parties are conservative parties wanting to uphold traditional ideas.

Suggested activities

- Reinforce what you said during the Starter activity by reading the first three paragraphs of the article 'Political parties and the political spectrum' (page 64). Write the terms 'ideology' and 'political spectrum' on the board and explain what they mean.

- Read the remainder of the article, and invite groups to study the article and to discuss the four questions on it (see 'In groups', page 64). Then ask them individually to write answers to the questions.

- Read the descriptions of British political parties on pages 65 and 66. Ask groups to study the key policies of the three main parties and discuss which policies they agree with.

- Ask groups to work out policies for a new political party, following the guidelines in the section 'Forming a political party' (page 66).

Plenary

Encourage representatives from each group to explain the policies of their new parties to the rest of the class.

Extension activities

Encourage individuals to use the internet to visit the websites of the British political parties to research what their current policies are on key issues.

Ask students to contact the constituency organisations of the main political parties to invite them to send a member to talk to the class. Before the visit, allow them to prepare some questions.

Assessment

Use Copymaster 21A to assess understanding of political parties and their policies.

Your Life 3/Year 9

UNIT 14 You and your opinions – which political party do you support?

Your Life 3/Year 9

Lesson 2 *Your Life 3*, page 67
National Curriculum Programme of Study for Citizenship coverage 1d, 1e, 1f, 2a, 2b, 2c, 3b; links with QCA exemplar units 6, 12

Objective: To examine what influences whether or not people vote and what decides who they vote for.

Resources

Copymaster 14 'Contemporary issues – where do you stand?' (*Your Life 3 Copymasters*, page 26)

Copies of Copymaster R12 'Developing as a citizen' (page 192)

Starter

Recap what the students found out about political parties in the previous lesson and talk about how, at general elections, political parties try to get people to vote for them by producing a manifesto (a statement of the policies they would follow if they were to form the government). Explain that in order to be able to choose between political parties, voters need to have thought through where they personally stand on the main issues of the day.

Suggested activities

- Ask students either to study the ten statements on page 67 or the 15 statements on Copymaster 14, to decide their opinion on each issue and to share their views in a group discussion, being prepared to change their minds if they find other people's arguments convincing.

- Ask: "What other issues are key issues that would determine how you would vote, if you were old enough to do so?" Invite the students to look again at the key policies of the three main parties (page 65) and to discuss in groups which party they would vote for, before individually writing about which party they would support and why.

- Read 'To vote or not to vote' (page 67). Ask groups to discuss the reasons why people may choose not to vote, then to debate which of the two statements they agree with and why (see 'In groups', page 67).

Plenary

Explain that in some countries voting at general elections is compulsory. Discuss with the class whether or not they think voting in UK general elections should be compulsory and hold a vote to decide what the class's view is.

Extension activity

Hold a mock election. Candidates could stand for either real political parties or the new political parties formed in the previous lesson. Ask groups to help candidates draft their manifestoes. Encourage the candidates to give speeches explaining their policies and to answer questions about their policies, then organise a secret ballot.

Recording and evaluating

Ask students to use the appropriate section of Copymaster R12 to help them to record and evaluate what they learned from this lesson.

UNIT 15 You and your body – safer sex, STIs and AIDS

Your Life 3/Year 9

Lesson 1 *Your Life 3*, pages 68–69
National Framework for PSHE coverage 2e

> **Objective:** To explain what safer sex means and to provide information about sexually transmitted infections.

Resources

Copies of Copymaster 15 'Sexually transmitted infections' (*Your Life 3 Copymasters*, page 27)

Starter

Explain that many young people have their first experience of sex without realising the risks involved and later regret it. Read '14-year-olds "regret having had sex"' (page 68). Explain that there is no such thing as totally safe sex; there's always some risk involved, which is why health experts use the term 'safer sex' rather than 'safe sex'.

Suggested activities

- Read 'What is safer sex?' (page 68) and discuss with the class the four rules for safer sex.

- Read 'Adolescents are at risk' and Anna's statement (page 68). Discuss why adolescents run a greater risk of getting an STI. Ask: "What do you think of Anna's boyfriend's attitude?" "Is his behaviour typical?" "What would you say to him to try to persuade him that his behaviour is unacceptable?"

- Read 'Sexually transmitted infections' and 'Chlamydia' (page 69). Reinforce what the article says by drawing up a list on the board of ten things young people should know about STIs and how to avoid them.

- Invite pairs to read 'What to do if you think you have an STI' (page 69), then to draft Lucy's reply to Sam (see 'For your file', page 69).

Plenary

Recap what the students have learned about STIs and what they should do if they think they have caught an STI by sharing some of their replies to Sam's letter.

Extension activities

Give out copies of Copymaster 15 and discuss with the class the detailed information it gives on the symptoms of STIs. Emphasise that while thrush and cystitis produce symptoms similar to some STIs, neither of them is sexually transmitted and both can be easily treated.

Your Life 3/Year 9

UNIT 15 You and your body – safer sex, STIs and AIDS

Your Life 3/Year 9

Lesson 2 *Your Life 3*, pages 70–71
National Framework for PSHE coverage 2e

Objective: To provide information about HIV and AIDS, and to explore attitudes to sex and AIDS.

Resources

Copies of Copymaster R10 'Keeping healthy' (page 190)

Starter

Ask groups to do a brainstorm and list what they know about HIV and AIDS. Then explain that while some of the things they have written down may be true, others may be false because there are a lot of myths about HIV and AIDS.

Suggested activities

- Invite the students in groups to study 'AIDS – the facts' (page 70) and to check whether the lists they made in the Starter activity were accurate. Then ask them to draw up a test-yourself quiz (see 'In groups', page 71) and to give the test to another group to do.

- Ask pairs to design a page for an internet website giving teenagers essential information on AIDS.

- Read the statements in the section 'Attitudes to sex' and 'Teenagers think HIV is "irrelevant"' (page 71). In groups, invite students to discuss the comments and the attitudes reported in the article and then to share their views in a class discussion.

Plenary

Ask the students to imagine they have to design an AIDS awareness poster to make young people realise that AIDS is a health issue they need to be concerned about. Discuss ideas on how they can get the message across, then ask them to design the posters.

Extension activity

Allow them to use the internet to find out further information about AIDS.

Recording and evaluating

Ask students to fill in the appropriate section of Copymaster R10 to record and evaluate what they learned from this unit.

UNIT 16 You as a citizen – of the world

Your Life 3/Year 9

Lesson 1 *Your Life 3*, pages 72–73
National Curriculum Programme of Study for Citizenship coverage 1i, 2a, 2b, 2c; links with QCA exemplar unit 10

Starter

Write the terms 'globalisation' and 'the global village' on the board. Explain what they mean and read the two introductory paragraphs and 'A global village' on page 72.

Suggested activities

- Read 'What are the causes of globalisation?' and 'Transnational corporations (TNCs)' (page 72). Discuss, as a class, the causes and effects of globalisation, then prompt the students, in groups, to discuss the three statements on page 72 (see 'In groups') before sharing their views with the rest of the class.

- Read 'The information superhighway' (page 73). Encourage groups to discuss the impact that the development of the internet has had so far. Ask: "What impact do you think it will have on people's lives in the future?" Then allow the students to share their ideas in a class discussion.

- Ask groups to read and discuss 'Problems of the internet' (page 73). Then allow them to share their views on the issues of control and censorship of the internet in a class discussion, before individually writing an article about the internet – its impact, its problems and its future (see 'For your file', page73).

Plenary

Recap what the students have learned about the causes and effects of globalisation by drawing two columns on the board labelled 'Causes' and 'Effects', and eliciting points from them in a class discussion. Ask the students to make copies for their files of the chart you draw up on the board.

Extension activity

Ask groups to carry out a survey of adults' views on the development of the internet by drafting questions to discover its impact on their lives, what they see as its problems and what they think should be done to control or censor it.

UNIT 16 You as a citizen – of the world

Your Life 3/Year 9

Lesson 2 *Your Life 3*, pages 74–75
National Curriculum Programme of Study for Citizenship coverage 1i, 2a, 2b, 2c; links with QCA exemplar unit 10

Objective: To understand the causes and effects of global warming and the measures that can be taken to reduce it.

Resources

Copies of Copymaster 16 'Unnatural disasters?' (*Your Life 3 Copymasters*, page 28)

Copies of Copymaster 22A 'Understanding global issues' (page 178)

Starter

Ask the students: "What do the terms 'global warming' and 'the greenhouse effect' mean?" Encourage them to help you draft definitions on the board. Then read the introductory paragraph on global warming and the two paragraphs on the greenhouse effect on page 74.

Suggested activities

- Ask individuals to read and make notes on 'Greenhouse gases' and 'The effects of global warming' (page 74), before discussing, in groups, what causes global warming and what its effects are.

- Allow pairs to read and discuss the three extracts on page 75, then to draft a letter to a newspaper expressing their concern about global warming and saying what they think the government should be doing about it.

- Ask the students, in groups, to read each other's letters, then to discuss what businesses and institutions, such as schools, can do to use energy more efficiently. Invite them to draft a series of questions about energy efficiency for the class representative to raise at the next school council meeting.

- Ask the class how energy conscious they are as individuals. What can individuals do to change their energy habits and reduce energy use? Then, on their own, ask them to design posters encouraging people to conserve energy.

Plenary

Ask: "If you were invited to put your views on global warming to an international conference on the issue, what would you say?" Make a list on the board of the points the students would want to make.

Extension activities

Ask groups to read and discuss the article on Copymaster 16. Then ask pairs to role play a journalist interviewing a Christian Aid spokesperson about what the report says.

Ask the students to use the internet to research global warming and the greenhouse effect by visiting websites such as the Friends of the Earth (www.foe.org.uk).

Assessment

Use Copymaster 22A to assess understanding of globalisation and global warming.

UNIT 16 You as a citizen – of the world

Your Life 3/Year 9

Lesson 3 *Your Life 3*, pages 76–77
National Curriculum Programme of Study for Citizenship coverage 1g, 1i, 2a, 2b, 2c; links with QCA exemplar units 10, 11, 13

Objective: To explore the role of the United Nations in keeping peace and to examine the arms trade.

Resources

Copies of Copymaster R12 'Developing as a citizen' (page 192)

Starter

Ask the students: "What do you know about the United Nations?" Explain that it was set up after the Second World War to try to keep peace in the world and to defend human rights, and that one of its key bodies is the UN Security Council. Read the introductory paragraph and the paragraph on the UN Security Council (page 76). Explain what a veto is.

Suggested activities

- Read 'A shattered dream' and 'Why has the UN failed to bring peace?' (page 76). Discuss with the class why the UN's attempts to bring peace to the world have largely failed.

- Study the information about the arms trade on page 77. Ask individuals to draw up a list of the main points entitled 'Five things you should know about the arms trade', then to compare their lists in groups.

- Read 'An ethical foreign policy' (page 77). Ask groups to discuss the two statements about the arms trade, then to share their views in a class discussion.

- Invite students to write their views on the arms trade and Britain's involvement in it.

Plenary

Ask pairs to say why they would or would not ever take part in a demonstration against Britain's involvement in the arms trade. Encourage them to share their views in a class discussion.

Extension activities

Ask students to find out more about the arms trade by visiting the website of the Campaign Against the Arms Trade (CAAT) at www.caat.org.uk.

Organise a debate on the motion 'This house believes that Britain should stop manufacturing and selling arms to anyone except our partners in the European Union'.

Recording and evaluating

Ask students to use the appropriate section of Copymaster R12 to record and evaluate what they learned from this unit.

Your Life 3/Year 9

UNIT 17 You and the community – pressure groups and campaigning

Your Life 3/Year 9

Lesson 1 *Your Life 3*, pages 78–79
National Curriculum Programme of Study for Citizenship coverage 1f, 1h, 2a, 2b, 2c; links with QCA exemplar unit 9

> **Objective:** To explore what pressure groups are and the techniques they use, and to examine how the Pedestrians Association campaigns to make walking safer.

Starter

Explain what a pressure group is. Give any examples of local pressure groups, together with examples of national pressure groups (e.g. League Against Cruel Sports, The Countryside Alliance) and international pressure groups (e.g. Amnesty International, Greenpeace). Then read the paragraphs explaining what pressure groups are (page 78).

Suggested activities

- Read 'Pressure group techniques' (page 78). Discuss with the class the different techniques that pressure groups use. Ask them to share their views on whether non-violent civil disobedience can ever be justified.

- Ask: "What do they think of pressure groups that are prepared to use violence?" Encourage them to write a statement saying why they agree or disagree with this opinion: 'Pressure groups should never resort to violence.' Then allow them to share their views in a class discussion.

- Invite groups to discuss issues about which they feel so strongly they would be prepared to campaign for them. Ask them to choose an issue from 'In groups' (top of page 78), and to explain the reasons for their choice in a class discussion.

- Read the article 'The Pedestrians Association' (page 75). Invite them to discuss in groups the hazards that the Pedestrians Association campaigns against and what particular hazards there are for pedestrians locally.

Plenary

Ask groups to report on the hazards for pedestrians which they have identified in your area.

Extension activities

Ask students to find out more about the Pedestrians Association by visiting their website (www.pedestrians.org.uk).

UNIT 17 You and the community – pressure groups and campaigning

Your Life 3/Year 9

Lesson 2 *Your Life 3*, pages 80–81
National Curriculum Programme of Study for Citizenship coverage 1f, 1h, 3b, 3c; links with QCA exemplar unit 9

Objective: To organise a campaign to make roads safer in your local area.

Resources

Copies of Copymaster 17 'Making residential roads safer' (*Your Life 3 Copymasters*, page 29)

Copies of Copymaster 23A 'Understanding how to organise an action group and run a campaign' (page 179)

Copies of Copymaster R12 'Developing as a citizen' (page 192)

Starter

Remind the students of what a pressure group is and the techniques they use. Draw a flowchart on the board, explaining the steps they will need to take to form a pressure group and mount a campaign. Step 1: Identify the problem and name the group; Step 2: Survey opinions; Step 3: Plan the campaign; Step 4: Produce materials, organise events and get media coverage; Step 5: Review strategy.

Suggested activities.

- Ask groups to identify a problem with traffic in your area. Use Copymaster 17 to help groups choose a street/streets in which there is a problem. Then invite them to present their ideas to the rest of the class. Discuss the ideas, agree on what the class is going to campaign for and choose a name for the group. Read 'Surveying opinions and collecting information' (page 80) and, in groups, ask students to draft a leaflet or questionnaire to survey other people's views.

- Hold a planning meeting and discuss what they would do as part of their campaign (see list in 'Planning your campaign', page 80). Read 'Hitting the headlines' (page 81). Discuss with the class the various ways of attracting media attention. Then study the press release and the helpful hints on page 81.

Plenary

Discuss what the students have learned about how to plan a campaign. If appropriate, appoint an organising committee to put their campaign into action.

Extension activities

Ask students to develop their campaign by first researching opinions to see if there is sufficient support for their point of view to make the campaign worthwhile. Then ask them to design and distribute a newsletter to get their message across. If appropriate, allow students to develop the campaign further by organising a petition and/or getting media coverage by sending out a press release. Discuss with the class how successful their campaign was and get them to write a statement reviewing how the campaign went (see 'For your file', page 81).

Assessment

Use Copymaster 23A to assess understanding of how to organise an action group and how to run a campaign.

Recording and evaluating

Ask students to use the appropriate section of Copymaster R12 to help them to record and evaluate what they learned from this unit.

UNIT 18 You and other people – people with mental illnesses

Your Life 3/Year 9

Lesson 1 *Your Life 3*, pages 82–83
National Framework for PSHE coverage 2c

Objective: To explain what mental illness is, to discuss attitudes towards it and learn how to cope with a mental illness in the family.

Starter

Write the terms 'mental illness' and 'mental handicap' on the board and explain that whereas mental illnesses can often be successfully treated, mental handicaps are disabilities, which affect a person permanently. People who are mentally handicapped may be born with a damaged brain or suffer brain damage in an accident. There are many sorts of mental illnesses which, like physical illnesses, can develop at any time during a person's life.

Suggested activities

● Read 'Mental illness – some questions and answers' (page 82). Label two columns on the board, 'Facts' and 'Myths', and use the information from the article to make lists of statements about mental illness that are true and false.

● Ask: "Why is it socially acceptable to be physically ill but less acceptable to be mentally ill?" Encourage the students, in groups, to discuss attitudes towards mental illness, then to share their views on the two questions on page 82 (see 'In groups') in a class discussion.

● Read 'Mental health problems' (page 83). Discuss with the class what they learn from it about how a person with mental illness may behave, how other family members can help them and how a young person might feel if a family member develops a mental illness.

Plenary

Invite the students, in pairs, to list the points they would make to try to reassure a friend who confides in them that she is feeling ashamed, upset and worried, because her mum has developed a mental illness. Encourage them to share their ideas in a class discussion.

Extension activity

Ask students to use the internet to find out more about mental illnesses. A useful site is the website of the Mental Health charity MIND (www.mind.org.uk).

UNIT 18 You and other people – people with mental illnesses

Objective: To explore the causes of mental illness.

Resources

Copies of Copymaster 18 'Types of mental illness' (*Your Life 3 Copymasters,* page 30)

Starter

Explain that mental illnesses are not 'caught' in the same way as physical illnesses. In many cases, there are several factors that trigger a mental illness. The main trigger may be a life-changing event like the death of a close relative or friend, the break-up of a relationship, or a serious accident. Whether or not a person develops a mental illness also depends on their personality.

Suggested activities

- Read 'What are the causes of mental illness?' (pages 84–85). Invite individuals to make notes, using the headings 'Physical causes', 'Social causes' and 'Environmental causes'. Then discuss, as a class, what they learned from the article about the different causes of mental illnesses.

- Discuss how mental illness is often triggered by stress. Encourage groups to discuss what pressures cause stress among teenagers and where these pressures come from, then to share their ideas in a class discussion.

- Read 'Odd or ill?' (page 85). Discuss with the class the difference between eccentricity and mental illness. Talk about the need to tolerate people's unusual behaviour so long as it does not interfere with other people's lives.

Plenary

Recap the main points made in the article about the causes of mental illness, stressing that as each individual case involves a different person, the triggers for the same mental illness are often different.

Extension activity

Give out copies of Copymaster 18 and discuss with the class the information it contains, before asking the students, in pairs, to test each other's knowledge of the different types. Ask them to read out the definitions one by one, while their partner names the illness.

UNIT 18 You and other people – people with mental illnesses

Your Life 3/Year 9

Lesson 3 *Your Life 3*, pages 86–87
National Framework for PSHE coverage 2c

> **Objective:** To understand what depression is and to discuss ways of dealing with depression.

Resources

Copies of Copymaster R11 'Developing relationships' (page 191)

Starter

Read the two introductory paragraphs on page 86 and discuss the difference between a mild form of depression and severe depression.

Suggested activities

- Read 'What you may be depressed about' (page 86). Ask the students in groups to discuss why teenagers get depressed and then to share their views in a class discussion.

- Read 'Symptoms of depression' (page 86). In pairs, ask students to draft the answer to a letter from Ria who has written to a magazine's agony aunt saying: 'I think my friend may be severely depressed. How can I tell?'

- Study 'How to defeat depression' and 'I'm feeling so depressed' (page 87). Invite groups to discuss the advice given in these articles about how to deal with depression. Ask: "What do you think are the three most useful pieces of advice?" Invite them to share their views in a class discussion.

- Ask the students to write an article for a teenage magazine about depression, its causes and how to deal with it.

Plenary

Re-emphasise the importance of getting help if you are severely depressed. Read 'Don't do it!' (page 86) and discuss with the class how they can get confidential help by contacting either the Samaritans or ChildLine if they are feeling desperate.

Recording and evaluating

Ask students to fill in the appropriate section of Copymaster R11 to record and evaluate what they learned from this unit.

UNIT 19 You and global issues – poverty

Your Life 3/Year 9

Lesson 1 *Your Life 3*, pages 88–89
National Curriculum Programme of Study for Citizenship coverage 1i, 2a, 2b, 3a; links with QCA exemplar unit 10

Objective: To understand what poverty is and to explore poverty and homelessness in the United Kingdom.

Starter

Explain that people who are regarded as very poor in a developed country may not be considered to be very poor in a developing country. Introduce the terms 'absolute poverty' and 'relative poverty', and explain them by reading the introductory paragraphs on page 88.

Suggested activities

- Read 'Who are the poor?' and 'Gap between rich and poor has grown' (page 88). Discuss with the class what they learn from these articles about who is poor in Britain today. Then discuss the view that the rich should pay more taxes to provide increased benefits for the poor (see 'In groups', page 88).

- Study 'Street life' (page 89). Ask the students, in pairs, to make notes on homelessness in Britain (the extent of the problem, its causes and ways of reducing the problem), before discussing, in groups, the view that homeless people have only got themselves to blame.

- Ask groups to discuss what can be done to reduce the problem of homelessness, before individually drafting a letter to their MP suggesting what the government should be doing to reduce it.

- Challenge students to write about living on the street from the point of view of a homeless teenager (see 'For your file', page 89). The writing could take the form of either a story, a letter, a poem or a song.

Plenary

Recap on which groups of people are the poorest in the UK today. Discuss the view that it's everyone's responsibility to help the poor and we shouldn't just leave it to the government. Ask: "Should people who can afford to do so give regular sums to charities which help the poor?" "What's your attitude towards beggars?" "Should you give money to beggars?"

Extension activity

Ask students to use the internet to find out more about homelessness in the UK. They can visit the websites of Shelter (www.shelter.org.uk) Crisis (www.crisis.org.uk) and Centrepoint (www.centrepoint.org.uk).

Your Life 3/Year 9

UNIT 19 You and global issues – poverty

Your Life 3/Year 9

Lesson 2 *Your Life 3*, pages 90–91
National Curriculum Programme of Study for Citizenship coverage 1i, 2a, 2b, 2c; links with QCA exemplar unit 10

Objective: To examine world poverty, exploring how the world is divided into rich and poor countries, and the effects of excessive consumption of resources by rich countries.

Starter

Read the two introductory paragraphs on page 90 and explain how the world can be broadly divided into the rich countries of the developed world (the North) and the poorer countries of the developing world (the South).

Suggested activities

- Read 'Differences between the North and the South' and 'Worlds apart from birth' (page 90). Ask the students, in pairs, to discuss the main differences between developed countries and developing countries and to make a copy of the chart for their files.

- Read 'Education and poverty' (page 90). Discuss with the class the link between education and poverty. Prompt them to imagine what their life might be like if they were living in poverty in a shanty town on the edge of a city in the developing world. Ask: "What would be the main differences from the life you lead as a teenager in Britain?"

- Study 'World's poor suffer as the rich destroy our planet' (page 91). Discuss, as a class, what they learn from the article about how the excessive consumption by rich countries is causing environmental damage and affecting the world's poorer nations. Then ask them to draft proposals for measures that will make people in rich countries cut down their consumption of essential resources. (See 'In groups', page 91).

Plenary

Ask representatives from each of the groups to share their ideas on what measures they suggest for getting people in the developed world to cut down their consumption. Discuss which measures would be most effective.

Your Life 3/Year 9

UNIT 19 You and global issues – poverty

Your Life 3/Year 9

Lesson 3 *Your Life 3*, pages 92–93
National Curriculum Programme of Study for Citizenship coverage 1f, 1i, 2a, 2b, 2c; links with QCA exemplar unit 10

Objective: To explore ways of ending the inequality between rich and poor countries and to explain what fair trade is.

Resources

Copies of Copymaster 19 'Fairtrade – your questions answered' (*Your Life 3 Copymasters*, page 31)

Copies of Copymaster 24A 'Understanding the global issues of poverty and inequality' (page 180)

Copies of Copymaster R12 'Developing as a citizen' (page 192)

Starter

Recap the differences discussed in the previous lesson between the rich and poor countries. Explain that cutting down consumption by rich countries is one measure that will help poorer countries, but that other measures need to be taken also.

Suggested activities

- Read 'How can we end the rich-poor divide' (page 92). Invite pairs to make notes of the measures suggested in the article, then encourage them to discuss, in groups, what can be done to reduce the inequalities that exist between the countries of the North and South.

- Study the article 'What is fair trade?' (page 93). Ask the students, in groups, to discuss the fair trade system and how it works. Then ask them to design and produce a leaflet explaining what fair trade is in order to try to persuade people to change their shopping habits and look for Fairtrade products.

- Challenge individuals to write a letter to a newspaper or to their MP expressing their views on the rich-poor divide.

Plenary

Prompt students to imagine they are an MP speaking in a debate in favour of a proposal to pay a tax of 0.1% of Britain's GNP to help eradicate poverty in developing countries. Ask: "What arguments would you use to try to persuade people to support the proposal?" Allow them to share their ideas as a class.

Extension activities

Further develop the students' understanding of fair trade by asking groups to study and discuss the information on Copymaster 19. They could use the internet to find out more about fair trade by contacting the Fairtrade Foundation website (www.fairtrade.org.uk).

Assessment

Use Copymaster 24A to assess understanding of global poverty and inequality.

Recording and evaluating

Ask students to use the appropriate section of Copymaster R12 to help them to record and evaluate what they learned from this unit.

Your Life 3/Year 9

UNIT 20 You and your achievements – reviewing your progress

Your Life 3/Year 9

Lesson 1 *Your Life 3*, pages 94–95
National Framework for PSHE coverage 1a; National Curriculum Programme of Study for Citizenship coverage 3c; links with QCA exemplar unit 19

Objective: To review your progress and achievements in Year 9, to set targets for Year 10 and to assess your study habits.

Resources

Copies of Copymaster 20 'How good are your study habits?' (*Your Life 3 Copymasters*, page 32).

Copies of Copymaster R9 'Understanding yourself' (page 189)

Starter

Explain that the lesson is the start of a four-step process: 1) Preparing your self-assessment; 2) Discussing your progress and achievements with your tutor; 3) Identifying and setting targets for Year 10; 4) Writing a statement for your Record of Achievement.

Suggested activities

- Read 'Preparing your self-assessment' (page 94). Then ask the students to follow the four steps and to draft statements commenting on their progress in their subjects and on their key skills, reviewing their achievements in their activities, and reflecting on their attitude and behaviour during the year.

- Use the quiz on Copymaster 20 to encourage the students to think about their study habits. Then ask pairs to read and discuss 'Assessing your study habits' (page 95), before writing a statement reflecting on their study habits and saying what they could do to improve them in Year 10.

Plenary

Allocate times for individuals to meet with you to discuss their statements and identify targets, allowing them further time (as necessary) to complete their statements.

Extension activities

Hold the discussion meetings with individuals. During the discussion, encourage them to note down any points you make (see 'Discussing your progress', page 94).

Ask students to draw up an action plan, setting targets for Year 10. (See 'Setting targets', page 94.)

Ask students to write a statement to put into their Record of Achievement (see 'Recording your achievements', page 94).

Recording and evaluating

Ask students to fill in the appropriate section of Copymaster R9 to record and evaluate what they learned from this unit.

1A Understanding your values

Draw up your list of ten rules for today. After each rule, write one or two sentences giving the reason why you believe that it is important for people to follow that rule.

Rule 1	
Reason	
Rule 2	
Reason	
Rule 3	
Reason	
Rule 4	
Reason	
Rule 5	
Reason	
Rule 6	
Reason	
Rule 7	
Reason	
Rule 8	
Reason	
Rule 9	
Reason	
Rule 10	
Reason	

2A Understanding children's rights

Use this quiz to check your knowledge of the laws about children's rights.

Decide which of these statements are true and which are false, and put a tick in one of the boxes.

	TRUE	FALSE
1. You can leave home without your parents' permission at 16.	☐	☐
2. Once you are 13 you can work for four hours on any day.	☐	☐
3. From the age of eight you can be held responsible for any crime you commit.	☐	☐
4. You need your parents' consent to join the armed forces if you are under 18.	☐	☐
5. At 16 you can buy yourself alcohol to drink with a meal in a pub or restaurant.	☐	☐
6. You have to be 21 before you can vote in a parliamentary or local election.	☐	☐
7. Your parents have no legal duty to give you pocket money.	☐	☐
8. Your parents have the right to smack you as hard and as often as they like.	☐	☐
9. Parents must take children's views into consideration when choosing a school for them.	☐	☐
10. Your parents can choose which religion you are brought up in.	☐	☐
11. Foster parents have all the same rights and responsibilities as natural parents.	☐	☐
12. Adopted children aged 14 and over have the right to see their birth records.	☐	☐

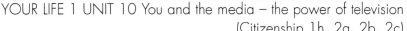

ASSESSMENT COPYMASTER

3A Understanding television

On a separate sheet, answer these questions as fully as you can, giving reasons for the statements you make and, wherever possible, supporting them with examples.

1. How much influence do you think television has on people's views and values: A little? Quite a lot? A huge amount?
   Give reasons for your view.
   (See 'Television and its influence' on page 48.)

2. Do you think television programmes present a fair and balanced view of all sections of society? Think about older people, people with disabilities and ethnic minorities, and give reasons for your views.
   (See 'TV isn't fair' on page 48.)

3. How true to life are TV soaps? In what ways are the characters and stories in soaps different from people and events in real life?
   (See 'How true to life are soaps' on page 49.)

4. How are the messages you get from the pictures you see in TV news broadcasts influenced by the viewpoint of the news reporter and what the reporter says?
   (See 'Every picture tells a story' on page 50.)

5. How can the camera angle from which a news picture is taken alter the message the picture gives?
   (See 'Viewpoint matters' on page 51.)

6. How does the point of view from which a drama or a comedy programme is presented influence your attitude towards the characters and their behaviour?
   (See 'The hero's point of view' on page 51.)

4A Understanding what being a good neighbour means

Draw up a list of ten 'Dos' and 'Don'ts' on how to behave in
order to be a good neighbour.

1	
2	
3	
4	
5	
6	
7	
8	
9	
10	

5A Assessing your speaking skills

On your own, think about your speaking skills. Rate each skill as either good, quite good or not very good. Then join up with a partner and discuss what your strengths and weaknesses are, and which skills you need to work on improving.

Taking part in group discussions

	Good	Quite good	Not very good
Joining in and contributing to the discussion	☐	☐	☐
Listening to what other people say	☐	☐	☐
Waiting your turn and not interrupting	☐	☐	☐
Supporting your views with reasons and examples	☐	☐	☐
Sticking to the subject	☐	☐	☐
Introducing new ideas	☐	☐	☐
Helping to keep the discussion focused	☐	☐	☐
Summarising ideas and opinions	☐	☐	☐
Reporting the group's views in a class discussion	☐	☐	☐

Making speeches

	Good	Quite good	Not very good
Starting with an introduction which grabs the audience's attention	☐	☐	☐
Developing your arguments and supporting them with reasons	☐	☐	☐
Arguing against opposite points of view	☐	☐	☐
Emphasising key points by varying your tone	☐	☐	☐
Keeping eye-contact with the audience	☐	☐	☐
Speaking clearly and loudly enough	☐	☐	☐
Speaking fluently and not too fast	☐	☐	☐
Standing up straight and using your body language to suggest confidence	☐	☐	☐
Using technical and visual aids to put points across	☐	☐	☐
Ending your speech with an emphatic conclusion	☐	☐	☐

On a separate sheet, write a statement saying what you have learned about your speaking skills from this activity, commenting on what your strengths are and which skills you need to work on improving in the future.

6A Understanding Parliament and Parliamentary elections

Choose the correct endings and write **a**, **b** or **c** in the box.

1. A general election has to be held at least once every
   a) 3 years
   b) 4 years
   c) 5 years
☐

2. You cannot vote until you are
   a) 16
   b) 17
   c) 18
☐

3. To vote, your name must appear
   a) on the electoral register
   b) in the local directory
   c) on a list of householders
☐

4. To become a candidate for election to Parliament, you must have your name put forward by
   a) a political party
   b) ten electors
   c) a local organisation
☐

5. You cannot stand for an MP unless
   a) you were born in the area
   b) live in the area
   c) are over 21
☐

6. Candidates stand for election to Parliament in areas known as parliamentary
   a) commissions
   b) communities
   c) constituencies
☐

7. You can vote in person by going to
   a) a local council office
   b) a polling station
   c) a party headquarters
☐

8. You put your completed voting slip in
   a) a budget box
   b) a ballot box
   c) a canvassing box
☐

9. The winning candidate is the person who
   a) gets more than 50% of the vote
   b) has more votes after first, second and third preferences are counted
   c) gets the most votes
☐

10. The number of MPs in the House of Commons is
   a) 501
   b) 587
   c) 659
☐

11. The leader of the party with a majority of MPs becomes
   a) the President
   b) the Prime Minister
   c) the Chancellor
☐

12. The group of senior ministers who meet to decide the government's policies is called
   a) the Cabinet
   b) the Governing Council
   c) the Steering Committee
☐

13. The minister in charge of the government's finances is called
   a) the Speaker
   b) the Chancellor of the Exchequer
   c) the Chief Whip
☐

14. A law, which is made by Parliament, is called
   a) a Bill
   b) a Referendum
   c) an Act of Parliament
☐

15. The House of Lords has
   a) more power than the House of Commons
   b) the same amount of power as the House of Commons
   c) less power than the House of Commons
☐

(7A) Understanding your values

Explain how to organise a fund-raising event for a charity by either writing a step-by-step guide or drawing a flowchart. Include advice on:

- how to decide what sort of fund-raising event to hold
- how to plan and organise the event
- how to present your donation to the charity
- how to review the project.

ASSESSMENT COPYMASTER

8A Understanding recycling

Complete this word puzzle to check your knowledge about recycling.

Clues across

1. The name of the political party whose main policies are to take care of the environment. (5)

2. Recycling schemes _ _ _ _ _ _ waste. (6)

4. Recycling schemes cut down the _ _ _ _ _ _ _ _ _ that results from burying waste in landfill sites. (9)

5. You can put your old newspapers in one at a recycling centre. (4)

6. Recycling uses less _ _ _ _ _ _ than producing things from new materials. (6)

9. Aluminium _ _ _ _ have a high scrap value. (4)

11. Soft drinks containers made of this can be recycled as filling in such things as sleeping bags. (7)

13. Waste can be burned in one. (11)

Clues down

1. Decaying waste in landfill sites produces _ _ _ _ _ such as methane. (5)

3. Recycling schemes help to _ _ _ _ _ _ _ _ the Earth's natural resources. (8)

4. Recycling this saves trees, by cutting down the amount of wood pulp that has to be imported to make it. (5)

7. Bottles made of this can be washed and reused or crushed and recycled. (5)

8. To reclaim things for further use. (7)

10. Saving energy by recycling reduces the release of gases that contribute to this sort of rain. (4)

12. Recycling steel cans means we use up less of the Earth's supply of _ _ _ _ ore. (4)

ASSESSMENT COPYMASTER

9A Understanding your values

Study the list of issues and rate how concerned you are about each one by putting a tick in the appropriate column.

	Concerned	Very concerned	Not concerned
Hunting			
Drugdealing			
Cloning			
AIDS			
Recycling			
World hunger			
Sex discrimination			
Experiments on live animals			
Pollution			
Euthanasia			
Racial prejudice			

Which three issues concern you the most? Write a statement saying which three issues you and most concerned about and why.

(10A) Understanding your rights

Use this quiz to test your knowledge of what rights the police have and what your rights are. Decide which of these statements are true and which are false, and put a tick in one of the boxes.

	TRUE	**FALSE**
1. If a police officer stops you in the street, you have the right to know why.	☐	☐
2. A police officer can stop you if they know you have been in trouble before.	☐	☐
3. If you are stopped in the street you must answer any questions which the police officer asks you.	☐	☐
4. If you are asked to go to a police station to help the police with their enquiries, you can refuse to go.	☐	☐
5. The police can search anyone who they think is behaving in an odd way.	☐	☐
6. If the police have a good reason for wanting to search you and you refuse to let them, you can be charged with obstruction.	☐	☐
7. Any kind of search must be carried out by a police officer who is the same sex as you.	☐	☐
8. The police can only detain you at a police station if you have been arrested.	☐	☐
9. You have the right to inform someone if you are being questioned at a police station.	☐	☐
10. The police cannot interview you without your parent's consent.	☐	☐
11. If you admit to an offence and it is your first offence, provided it is not too serious, you will get a reprimand.	☐	☐
12. If you break the law a second time, you will automatically be prosecuted, however minor the offence is.	☐	☐
13. If the police believe you have committed an offence, they can give you a reprimand or a warning, even if you do not admit the offence.	☐	☐
14. If you are reprimanded, warned or charged by the police, they will take your fingerprints and a photo of you.	☐	☐
15. Records of your offences are kept on the Police National Computer for five years.	☐	☐

ASSESSMENT COPYMASTER

11A Understanding advertising

Complete this word puzzle to check your knowledge about advertising.

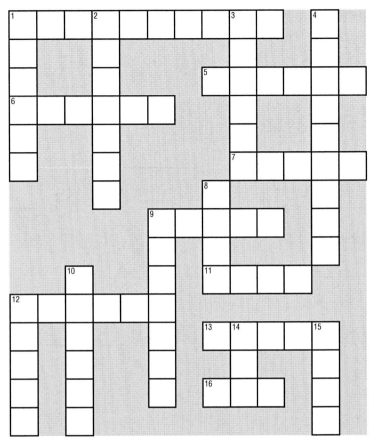

Clues across

1. A standardised image of a particular type of person often used by advertisers. (10)

5. A catchy, little rhyme or verse used in an advert. (6)

6. All advertisements broadcast on TV and radio must be legal, _ _ _ _ _ _ _, honest and truthful. (6)

7. A _ _ _ _ _, such as football, attracts a lot of sponsorship from advertisers, because it is so popular. (5)

9. Adverts for _ _ _ _ _ foods must not suggest that such products may be substituted for balanced meals. (5)

11. A trademark or company emblem printed on a piece of clothing as a way of advertising. (4)

12. A short, snappy, easy-to-remember phrase used in an advertisement. (6)

13. All advertisements broadcast on TV must be _ _ _ _ _, decent, honest and truthful. (5)

16. The Independent Television Commission which regulates all advertisements that appear on TV. (1,1,1)

Clues down

1. TV adverts aimed at children under 12 are banned in this country. (6)

2. Most of the _ _ _ _ _ _ _ of TV companies, newspapers and magazines comes from the money that advertisers pay them. (7)

3. _ _ _ _ _ _ of products advertised to children must not be minimised by words such as 'only' or 'just'. (6).

4. What we call a famous person who uses their name to endorse a product. (9)

8. Advertisements to children must not invite them to purchase products by telephone or _ _ _ _. (4)

9. To pay money for your company's name to be promoted, e.g. by a team or an individual, or for it to be associated with a sporting event. (7)

10. All advertisements broadcast on TV and radio must legal, decent, _ _ _ _ _ _ and truthful. (6)

12. These increase as a result of a successful advertising campaign. (5)

14. Advertisements to children must not encourage them to do this frequently throughout the day. (3)

15. Advertisements must not _ _ _ _ children to believe that unless they have or use a product they are inferior. (4)

12A Understanding how to organise a social event

Draw up a checklist of things you would need to do when planning and organising a disco for your Year group. Include advice on such things as:

- choosing a date
- choosing and booking the venue
- finding and booking a DJ
- printing and selling the tickets
- organising and selling refreshments
- organising adult support and supervision
- arranging clearing up after the event.

(13A) Understanding the difference between facts and opinions

Study the list of statements below and decide which are FACTS and which are OPINIONS. Put a cross in the appropriate box.

	FACT	OPINION
1. Gambling is a waste of time and money.	☐	☐
2. People can become addicted to gambling.	☐	☐
3. If you get your skin tattooed, you will regret it.	☐	☐
4. It is against the law to tattoo someone under the age of 18.	☐	☐
5. People who smoke are likely to die earlier than non-smokers.	☐	☐
6. Smoking should be banned in public places.	☐	☐
7. Foxhunting is cruel and unnecessary.	☐	☐
8. Foxhunting is a way of controlling the number of foxes.	☐	☐
9. People who are found guilty of serious crimes are often sent to prison.	☐	☐
10. Tougher prison sentences would reduce the amount of crime.	☐	☐

(14A) Understanding the European Union

Complete this crossword puzzle to check your knowledge of the European Union.

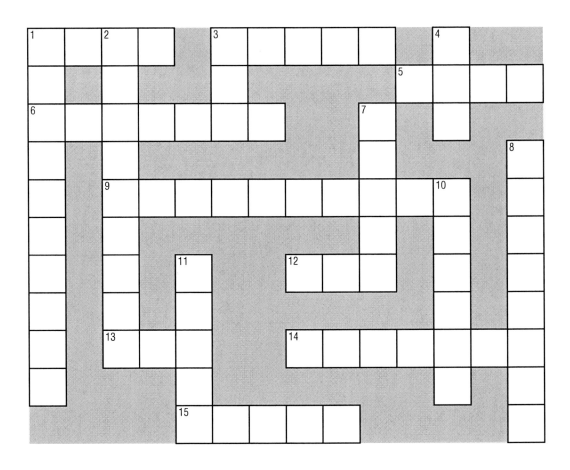

Clues across

1. In 1957, the European Economic Community (EEC) was set up by the Treaty of _ _ _ _. (4)

3. The EEC made it easier for member countries to _ _ _ _ _ with each other by abolishing tariffs. (5)

5. The single currency is called the _ _ _ _. (4)

6. This Scandinavian country joined the EU in 1995. (7)

9. The European Parliament meets in this city. (10)

12. A country which puts more money into the EU budget than it takes out is called a _ _ _ contributor. (3)

13. The number of states which set up the EEC in 1957. (3)

14. The EU's main decision-making body is the _ _ _ _ _ _ _ of the European Union. (7)

15. This country joined the EEC in 1986. (5)

Clues down

1. In 1975 the British people voted in a _ _ _ _ _ _ _ _ _ _ to remain in the EEC. (10)

2. Proposals for new laws are discussed by government _ _ _ _ _ _ _ _ _ from each of the member states. (9)

3. The number of new states which joined the EU in 2004. (3)

4. The UKIP would like to take Britain _ _ _ of the EU. (3)

7. European laws are interpreted by the European _ _ _ _ _ of Justice. (5)

8. The cleanest beaches in Europe are allowed to fly this. (4,4)

10. This country joined the EEC in 1981. (6)

11. Those in favour of a federal Europe want to see _ _ _ _ _ harmonised and a common foreign policy adopted. (5)

(15A) Understanding Local Agenda 21

Check your understanding of Local Agenda 21 by completing this word puzzle.

1. One of the aims of Local Agenda 21 is to cut down the damage caused to air, water and soil by _ _ _ _ _ _ _ _ _. (9)

2. Local Agenda 21 is an initiative by local _ _ _ _ _ _ _. (8)

3. Local Agenda 21 encourages _ _ _ _ _ _ _ _ _ schemes whereby materials are collected so that they can be used again. (9)

4. 5. Local Agenda 21 promotes

_ _,
which means meeting our present needs without affecting the ability of future generations to meet their needs. (11, 11)

6. Local Agenda 21 aims to make people do things like turn off taps so that they don't _ _ _ _ _ water. (5)

7. Local Agenda 21 aims to get people to turn off lights and other electrical equipment so that they will save _ _ _ _ _ _. (6)

8. Local Agenda 21 gets people to think about how we are using the world's _ _ _ _ _ _ _ _ _ faster than they can be replaced. (9)

9. Local Agenda 21 is designed to protect the _ _ _ _ _ _ _ _ _ _ _ from being damaged by human activities. (11)

10. Local Agenda 21 aims to get people to _ _ _ _ _ _ the amount of materials they use which cannot be replaced. (6)

11. Local Agenda 21 aims to get everyone to take responsibility for the problems which the _ _ _ _ _ is facing. (5)

16A Understanding world hunger

Below are some reasons that people give to explain why many of the people in sub-Saharan Africa do not get enough to eat. Put a tick beside those reasons that you agree with and a cross beside those reasons that you disagree with.

	Agree	Disagree
1. People in Africa are lazy.	☐	☐
2. The best land is used for cash crops for export.	☐	☐
3. There is not enough food produced in the world.	☐	☐
4. People have too many children.	☐	☐
5. Nothing grows in Africa, because it's all desert.	☐	☐
6. Farmers are too poor to buy the seeds and tools they need.	☐	☐
7. Some people in the world get more than their fair share of food.	☐	☐
8. African farmers are not given a fair deal on the world market.	☐	☐
9. Drought and famine are natural disasters which cannot be prevented.	☐	☐
10. Governments spend money on buying arms and fighting wars, which could otherwise be spent on developing agriculture.	☐	☐

Write a paragraph explaining the real reasons for why there is hunger in sub-Saharan Africa.

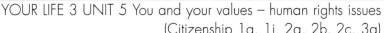

(17A) Understanding human rights

Check your understanding of human rights by completing this word puzzle.

Down (HUMAN RIGHTS):

1 H
2 U
3 M
4 A
5 N

6 R
7 I
8 G
9 H
10 T
11 S

1. Everyone has the right to have a _ _ _ _ to live in. (4)

2. The _ _ _ _ _ _ _ _ _ Declaration of Human Rights was drawn up in 1948. (9)

3. _ _ _ _ _ _ _ International is a group that campaigns against human rights abuses. (7)

4. The town in France where the European Court of Human Rights was set up. (10)

5. Forty-four countries have passed laws against domestic _ _ _ _ _ _ _ _. (8)

6. Women's rights in the UK are protected by the Sex _ _ _ _ _ _ _ _ _ _ _ _ _ _ acts. (14)

7. Anyone who is arrested and held in prison has the right to a fair _ _ _ _ _. (5)

8. Everyone has the right to freedom of _ _ _ _ _ _ _, conscience and religion. (7)

9. The rights of young people are set out in a separate convention on the rights of the _ _ _ _ _. (5)

10. People who use _ _ _ _ _ _ _ to extract information from a prisoner are abusing the prisoner's human rights. (7)

11. Anyone who refuses to fight in the armed forces is known as a _ _ _ _ _ _ _ _ _ _ _ _ _ objector. (13)

(18A) Understanding crimes and punishments
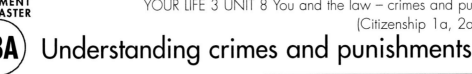

On a separate sheet, answer these questions as fully as you can, giving reasons for your views.

1. What do you think are the main reasons why so many young people commit crimes?

2. Why do you think girls today are more likely to commit crimes than girls of 50 years ago?

3. How serious an offence do you think shoplifting is?

4. Should shopkeepers always call the police if they catch someone shoplifting?

5. What do you think should be the main aims of a punishment given to someone found guilty of a criminal offence?

6. For which criminal offences do you think a person should always receive a custodial sentence?

7. What alternative punishments are there to prison sentences? Give examples of cases in which you think these punishments should be given rather than prison sentences.

8. Do you think monitoring young offenders is a good way of reducing crime? Give reasons for your answer and say what measures you think would be most effective in cutting down crime.

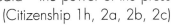

(19A) Understanding the press

On a separate sheet, answer these questions as fully as you can, giving reasons for any views you express.

1. What is a free press? How important do you think it is to have a free press?
(See 'The power of the government' on page 48.)

2. What is a newspaper proprietor? Is it right that a proprietor should have so much control over the political message of a newspaper?
(See 'The power of the owners' on page 48.)

3. Explain what the term 'spin-doctoring' means. How do political parties try to manage the news?
(See 'News management' on page 48.)

4. How is the content of newspapers influenced by a) consumer demand and b) advertisers?
(See 'Who controls the content of newspapers?' on page 49.)

5. Explain what the term 'news value' means. Who decides how much space a story should be given in a newspaper?
(See 'Who controls the content of newspapers?' on page 49.)

6. Do people have the right to know about the private lives of public figures? Or do public figures have a right to privacy in their private lives? When does media interest become an invasion of privacy?
(See 'Public interest versus private rights' on page 49.)

(20A) Understanding local government

1. What is a unitary authority?

2. Which local authority services are county councils responsible for?

3. Which local authority services are district councils responsible for?

4. What is the council tax?

5. Why are some people in favour of replacing the council tax with a local income tax?

6. What are the two other main sources of income for local councils besides the council tax?

7. Who can stand for election to the local council?

8. How long is a local councillor elected for?

9. Explain what a local councillor does.

ASSESSMENT COPYMASTER

YOUR LIFE 3 – UNIT 14 You and your opinions – Which political party do you support? (Citizenship 1d, 1e, 1f, 2a, 2b, 2c, 3b)

(21A) Understanding political parties and their policies

1. Study the information on the three main political parties on page 65.
   Think about each area of policy, decide which party's policy you
   support, tick the appropriate box, and say why.

Education	Labour ☐	Conservative ☐	Liberal Democrats ☐
Health services	Labour ☐	Conservative ☐	Liberal Democrats ☐
Taxation	Labour ☐	Conservative ☐	Liberal Democrats ☐
Electoral reform	Labour ☐	Conservative ☐	Liberal Democrats ☐
Europe	Labour ☐	Conservative ☐	Liberal Democrats ☐

2. Would you vote in the next general election, if you were old enough to do so?   Yes/No

   Explain why you would or would not vote.

3. If voting was compulsory, and you were old enough to vote, which
   party would you vote for? Explain why. (Remember – you could vote
   for one of the fringe parties rather than one of the three main parties.)

22A Understanding global issues

Answer these questions as fully as you can. If necessary, continue on a separate sheet.

Globalisation (see pages 72–73)

1. What do you understand by the term 'globalisation'?

2. What are the main causes of globalisation?

3. What do you think are the main effects of globalisation?

Global warming (see pages 74–75)

4. What is global warming?

5. What has caused global warming?

6. What are the effects of global warming?

7. How can global warming be reduced?

23A **Understanding how to organise an action group and run a campaign**

Explain how to organise an action group on a local issue and how to run a campaign by either writing a step-by-step guide or drawing up a list of tips. Include advice on:

- how to find out if there is enough support to form an action group
- how to set up the action group
- how to plan the campaign
- how to communicate information about what the action group is doing
- how to draw the attention of local politicians to the action group and its purpose
- how to use the media to gain publicity for the campaign.

(24A) Understanding the global issues of poverty and inequality

Answer these questions as fully as you can. If necessary, continue on a separate sheet.

1. What are the main differences between the rich countries of the North and the poor countries of the South? (See 'Differences between the North and the South' on page 90.)

2. How are education and poverty linked? (See 'Education and poverty' on page 90.)

3. How does excessive consumption by the world's rich countries cause problems for the world's poor countries? (See 'World's poor suffer as the rich destroy our planet' on page 91.)

4. What actions do you think we should take in order to end the rich-poor divide? Should we: Write off third world debt? Increase the amount of aid to poor countries? Share out trade by taxation? Develop more fair trade schemes? Say which measures you think would be most effective and why. (See 'How can we end the rich-poor divide?' and 'What is fair trade?' on pages 92–93.)

R/E COPY MASTER

 R1) **Understanding yourself**

Use this sheet to reflect on the knowledge and skills you learned from these units, and on how useful the units were in helping you to decide what you think and feel about the topics you discussed.

What did you learn...

1. about how to manage your anxieties and worries and how to cope with feelings of rejection, shyness and grief?
   (Unit 1 – PSHE 1d)

2. about how to manage your time and how to handle your homework?
   (Unit 4 – PSHE 1a)

3. about how to handle your money and how to budget?
   (Unit 11 – PSHE 1g)

4. about your progress in Year 7, your strengths and weaknesses and areas you need to focus on developing in the future?
   (Unit 20 – PSHE 1a; Citizenship 3c)

List the main reasons why you found these units helpful.

I found the units helpful because...

R2 / Keeping healthy

Use this sheet to reflect on the knowledge and skills you learned from the Keeping Healthy units, and on how useful the units were in helping you to decide what you think and feel about these health issues.

What did you learn...

1. about the physical and emotional changes that occur during puberty and how to manage them?
(Unit 2 – PSHE 2a)

2. about the potential risks from smoking and passive smoking and how to resist the pressure to smoke?
(Unit 7 – PSHE 2b, 2d, 2g)

3. about illegal drugs and the dangers of drug abuse?
(Unit 12 – PSHE 2d)

4. about what a healthy diet is, the importance of exercise and about people's attitudes to their body shapes?
(Unit 15 – PSHE 2a, 2b, 2c, 2f)

List the main reasons why you found these units helpful.

I found the units helpful because...

Your Life KS3 Co-ordinator's File © HarperCollins*Publishers* Ltd 2005. This page may be photocopied for use in the classroom.

R3) Developing relationships

Use this sheet to reflect on the knowledge and skills you learned from these units, and on how useful the units were in helping you to decide what you think and feel about the topics you discussed.

What did you learn...

1. about how people from different communities have different beliefs and about their dress customs, food customs and different religious festivals? (Unit 3 – Citizenship 1b)

2. about the causes of conflict within families, about the need to see other people's points of view, and about how to resolve problems with parents and brothers and sisters? (Unit 6 – PSHE 3e, 3g, 3h, 3i)

3. about the different forms of bullying – how it feels, why people do it and how to deal with it? (Unit 9 – PSHE 1b, 3a, 3j)

4. about what disability means, what it is like to have a disability and how to meet the needs of people with disabilities so that they are not discriminated against? (Unit 18 – PSHE 3a, 3b; Citizenship 3a)

List the main reasons why you found these units helpful.

I found the units helpful because...

R/E COPY MASTER

R4) Developing as a citizen

Use the questions on this sheet to reflect on the knowledge and skills you learned from the Citizenship units, and on how useful the units were in helping you to decide what you think and feel about the topics you discussed.

Write your answers on a separate sheet.

What did you learn ...

1. about what actions are considered to be right and wrong and why behaviour codes are necessary?
   (Unit 5 – Citizenship 1a, 1b, 2a, 2b, 2c)

2. about the laws concerning young people: parents' responsibilities and duties, children's rights and child employment laws?
   (Unit 8 – Citizenship 1a, 1f, 2a, 2b, 2c, 3a)

3. about the influence of television, and how to recognise bias and viewpoints in television programmes?
   (Unit 10 – Citizenship 1h, 2a, 2b, 2c)

4. about what being a good neighbour involves, how to decide what would improve your neighbourhood and how to take community action to improve it?
   (Unit 13 – Citizenship 1c, 1g, 2a, 2b, 2c, 3a, 3b)

5. about how to communicate rational arguments, listening to and contributing to discussions, making speeches and expressing your opinions in letters, articles and essays?
   (Unit 14 – Citizenship 2a, 2b, 2c)

6. about how laws are made, how central government is structured, what happens in Parliament and how MPs are elected?
   (Unit 16 – Citizenship 1a, 1c, 1d, 1e, 2a, 2b, 2c)

7. about how to work co-operatively to choose a charity to support and how to decide on and to plan a fundraising activity?
   (Unit 17 – Citizenship 1f, 2a, 3b)

8. about the need to reduce waste, the benefits of recycling and how to work together to develop a school recycling scheme?
   (Unit 19 – Citizenship 1i, 2a, 2b, 2c, 3b)

List the main reasons why you found these units helpful.

> I found the units helpful because...

R/E COPY MASTER

R5 Understanding yourself

Use this sheet to reflect on the knowledge and skills you learned from these units, and on how useful the units were in helping you to decide what you think and feel about the topics you discussed.

What did you learn...

1. about what self-esteem is and why it is important, and about how to develop self-confidence and how to learn from your mistakes?
(Unit 1 – PSHE 1a, 1c, 2a, 3c)

2. about gambling, the problems it can cause and what responsible gambling is?
(Unit 4 – PSHE 1g)

3. about how to use your leisure time constructively and why it is important to get enough exercise?
(Unit 11 – PSHE 1a, 2c)

4. about your progress and achievements in Year 8 and how to set targets for the future?
(Unit 20 – PSHE 1a; Citizenship 3c)

List the main reasons why you found these units helpful.

I found the units helpful because...

R6 / Keeping healthy

Use this sheet to reflect on the knowledge and skills you learned from the Keeping Healthy units and on how useful the units were in helping you to decide what you think and feel about these health issues.

What did you learn...

1. about the risks of drugtaking, the laws about drugs and how to deal with pressure to experiment with drugs?
   (Unit 2 – PSHE 2a, 2d, 2g)

2. about safety and how to give emergency first aid at home and on the roads, and about child abuse and how to stay safe on the street?
   (Unit 7 – PSHE 2f, 2g, 2h)

3. about alcohol and its effects and the problems alcohol can cause people?
   (Unit 12 – PSHE 2d, 2f)

4. about contraception and safer sex and what is acceptable and unacceptable behaviour in a relationship?
   (Unit 15 – PSHE 2e)

List the main reasons why you found these units helpful.

I found the units helpful because...

R/E COPY MASTER

R7 Developing relationships

Use this sheet to reflect on the knowledge and skills you learned from these units, and on how useful the units were in helping you to decide what you think and feel about the topics you discussed.

What did you learn...

1. about the diversity of British society, about ethnic stereotyping and about how ethnic minorities are presented in the media?
(Unit 3 – PSHE 3a; Citizenship 1b, 1h, 2a, 3a)

2. about the feelings people experience when parents separate or divorce and about how to cope with the changes that result?
(Unit 6 – PSHE 1d, 3e, 3f, 3g)

3. about friendship – what makes a good friend, how to make and keep friends, how friends may influence you and how to resist peer pressure?
(Unit 9 – PSHE 3b, 3c, 3i, 3j, 3k)

4. about what ageism is and the problems older people may face, and about the changing age-profile of society and the implications of the increasing number of older people?
(Unit 18 – PSHE 3a, 3b; Citizenship 2a, 2b, 2c, 3a)

List the main reasons you found these units helpful.

I found the units helpful because...

R8) Developing as a citizen

Use the questions on this sheet to reflect on the knowledge and skills you learned from the Citizenship units, and on how useful the units were in helping you to decide what you think and feel about the topics you discussed.

Write your answers on a separate sheet.

What did you learn...

1. about what influences your beliefs and values, about whom you admire and why, and about which social and environmental issues concern you the most?
   (Unit 5 – Citizenship 2a, 2b, 2c)

2. about the role of the police, their duties and powers, and the system for dealing with young offenders, and about people's attitudes to the police?
   (Unit 8 – Citizenship 1a, 2a, 2b, 2c)

3. about the power and influence of advertising, the rules governing it and the techniques advertisers use?
   (Unit 10 – Citizenship 1h, 2a, 2b)

4. about the school as a community and how as a member of Year 8 you can participate in the school community?
   (Unit 13 – Citizenship 1a, 1c, 1f, 2a, 2b, 2c, 3b)

5. about how to form opinions on social and environmental issues and how to present and justify your opinions in discussions and debates?
   (Unit 14 – Citizenship 2a, 2b, 2c)

6. about the development and organisation of the European Union, what it means to be a citizen of the European Union and about Britain's relationship with the European Union?
   (Unit 16 – Citizenship 1i, 2a, 2b, 2c)

7. about the need to respect the environment, the importance of sustainability and how to develop group activities to improve the school environment and the local environment?
   (Unit 17 – Citizenship 1c, 1f, 2a, 3b, 3c)

8. about global issues concerning food production, food shortages and famine and the lack of fresh clean water in many areas and how the basic needs of many of the world's population go unmet?
   (Unit 19 – Citizenship 1i, 2a, 2b, 2c, 3a)

List the main reasons why you found these units helpful.

I found the units helpful because...

R9 Understanding yourself

Use this sheet to reflect on the knowledge and skills you learned from these units, and on how useful the units were in helping you to decide what you think and feel about the topics you discussed.

What did you learn...

1. about decision-making – what influences your decision-making, how to make your own decisions and how to deal with peer pressure?
(Unit 3 – PSHE 1a, 3i, 3j)

2. about the feelings of loss you experience when someone dies or a relationship breaks up, how to cope with feelings of grief and of rejection and how to support others who are experiencing such feelings?
(Unit 6 – PSHE 1d, 3c, 3e)

3. about how bank accounts can help you to handle your money and about the advantages of different forms of saving?
(Unit 11 – PSHE 1g)

4. about your progress and achievements in Year 9, the strengths and weaknesses of your study habits and how you could improve your study habits?
(Unit 20 – PSHE 1a; Citizenship 3c)

List the main reasons why you found these units helpful.

I found the units helpful because...

R10 Keeping healthy

Use this sheet to reflect on the knowledge and skills you learned from the Keeping Healthy units, and on how useful the units were in helping you to decide what you think and feel about these health issues.

What did you learn...

1. about how your personality develops during adolescence, and how to recognise and deal with your feelings and moods?
   (Unit 1 – PSHE 1a, 1c, 1d, 2a, 2c, 3e)

2. about the risks involved in drugtaking, the problems drugs can cause and what to do in an emergency caused by drugtaking?
   (Unit 7 PSHE 2d, 2h)

3. about media pressure to be a particular body shape, and about the eating disorders anorexia nervosa and bulimia?
   (Unit 12 – PSHE 2b, 2f)

4. about the risks of early sexual activity, sexually transmitted infections and HIV/AIDS and what safer sex is?
   (Unit 15 – PSHE 2e)

List the main reasons why you found these units helpful.

I found the units helpful because...

R11) Developing relationships

Use this sheet to reflect on the knowledge and skills you learned from these units, and on how useful the units were in helping you to decide what you think and feel about the topics you discussed.

What did you learn...

1. about racism and racial discrimination, about why some people are racist and about how to take a stand against racism?
(Unit 2 – PSHE 3a, 3b, 3j, 3k; Citizenship 1b, 2a, 3a)

2. about your rights and responsibilities within your family, the causes of tensions between teenagers and parents and how to deal with arguments?
(Unit 4 – PSHE 3e, 3g, 3h, 3i, 3k)

3. about what being assertive means and assertiveness techniques?
(Unit 9 – PSHE 1b, 1c, 3a, 3i, 3k)

4. about what mental illness is and what causes it, and about how to recognise and deal with depression?
(Unit 18 – PSHE 2c)

List the main reasons why you found these units helpful.

I found the units helpful because...

R12 Developing as a citizen

Use the questions on this sheet to reflect on the knowledge and skills you learned from the Citizenship units, and on how useful the units were in helping you to decide what you think and feel about the topics you discussed.

Write your answers on a separate sheet.

What did you learn...

1. about basic human rights, about how they are frequently violated and what Amnesty International is and does, and about women's rights and discrimination against women?
(Unit 5 – PSHE 3a; Citizenship 1a, 1f, 1i, 2a, 2b, 2c, 3a)

2. about crime, its consequences for the victim and the offender, about different types of punishment and their aims and about actions being taken to reduce youth crime?
(Unit 8 – Citizenship 1a, 2a, 2b, 2c)

3. about the power of the press, about what controls the content of newspapers and teenage magazines and about how young people are presented in the press?
(Unit 10 – Citizenship 1h, 2a, 2b, 2c)

4. about the structure of local government, the services local authorities provide and the importance of taking an interest in local affairs?
(Unit 13 – Citizenship 1c, 2a, 3b, 3c)

5. about political parties and what they stand for and why it is important to vote?
(Unit 14 – Citizenship 1d, 1e, 1f, 2a, 2b, 2c, 3b)

6. about what globalisation is and its impact, and about the causes and effects of global warming and what steps need to be taken to reduce it?
(Unit 16 – Citizenship 1g, 1i, 2a, 2b, 2c)

7. about pressure groups and the techniques they use and about how to organise a campaign on a local issue?
(Unit 17 – Citizenship 1f, 1h, 2a, 2b, 2c, 3b, 3c)

8. about poverty and the impact of the unequal distribution of wealth between countries and about what fair trade means?
(Unit 19 – Citizenship 1f, 1i, 2a, 2b, 2c, 3a)

List the main reasons why you found these units helpful.

I found the units helpful because...